A COMPLIMENT TO YOU

Edited by

Natalie Nightingale

First published in Great Britain in 2001 by
POETRY NOW
Remus House,
Coltsfoot Drive,
Peterborough, PE2 9JX
Telephone (01733) 898101
Fax (01733) 313524

HB ISBN 0 75432 700 0
SB ISBN 0 75432 701 9

FOREWORD

Although we are a nation of poets we are accused of not reading poetry, or buying poetry books. After many years of listening to the incessant gripes of poetry publishers, I can only assume that the books they publish, in general, are books that most people do not want to read.

Poetry should not be obscure, introverted, and as cryptic as a crossword puzzle: it is the poet's duty to reach out and embrace the world.

The world owes the poet nothing and we should not be expected to dig and delve into a rambling discourse searching for some inner meaning.

The reason we write poetry (and almost all of us do) is because we want to communicate: an ideal; an idea; or a specific feeling. Poetry is as essential in communication, as a letter; a radio; a telephone, and the main criterion for selecting the poems in this anthology is very simple: they communicate.

CONTENTS

SIX LONG DAYS

Monday, I was told you had only days to live
I could not take it in, I knew that you were frail,
My beautiful mum, my precious jewel,
Lying there in your hospital bed, so tiny, so pale.

Tuesday, we talked and you said you were really, really ill,
You had something very important to tell me,
But you could not find the strength to say the words,
And I can only wonder as now you never will.

Wednesday, the pain was so intense you could not be at ease,
Morphine was administered, the pain to appease,
You cried, 'Don't go, leave me never,'
I replied, 'I will stay with you always and forever.'

Thursday, I played your favourite song and spoke of love,
I prayed for your release to God in Heaven above,
You were so tiny, like a beautiful little doll,
Your skin was like cream satin I do recall.

Friday, you seemed to shrink with each passing minute,
You opened your eyes so dark as if to commit to memory,
Your dearly loved ones in the ward,
The world, and all the wonders in it.

Saturday, the sound of your laboured breathing,
So loud it filled every crevice within the room,
Then the deathly silence that announced to all
That you, my magnificent, marvellous mum were finally leaving.

Sleep with the angels Mum.

Linda Lawton

NURSE

Thank you for caring, for all the hours
Comforting patients, arranging flowers
Night-time shifts, tenderness given
Selfless, courageous, altruism
Mopping patients brows, stitching neatly
Being ever so tired, but smiling sweetly
For meting out, prescribed medication
Defining the word, dedication
Here's to you, nurses of action
Relieving people, stuck in traction
Working hard, through the night
Showing sympathy, to those in plight
Dealing with trauma and disaster
Taking to surgery, on silent castor
People in need of medical aid
And all for what? So you can be paid
After grafting, sweating
Giving your all
Signing for admittance
A pittance
For answering the call.

Danny Coleman

TO MY LOVE

There are not enough words to say
Thank you for all that you do
You are there for me every day
Your love has always remained true.

Through the good times and bad
We've stayed strong
Even when I've made you mad
You've never gone.

You make each day special for me
Just having you near is a dream
This is how life should always be
No matter how hard it may seem.

A love like ours
Is real and true to life
It can't always be hearts and flowers
I am so proud to be your wife.

Dawn Harrison

CUP OF LOVE

My auntie lived beside the sea,
she lived with my grandma and me.
The magic of the sun and sand,
the memory of the tender hand.
Picnics in the countryside
picking bluebells that soon died.
Life was good and love was there
each time I needed gentle care.
As years passed by and I grew up
I needed to drink from the cup
of memories of happy years
to stop the pain and dry the tears.
And now I sit beside the bed
and gently stroke the little head
of beauty sleeping warm and snug
and know she'll wake up to a hug.
I'll take her hand and walk the way
my auntie took me to the bay.
I'll stack her memory full of plenty
and fill her cup so it's never empty.

Brenda Weir

MOTHER LOVE

This is a tribute, to a very special mother,
She hasn't got a sister, or an older brother,
But her very existence, makes our lives complete,
For she controls the coolness, and the welcome heat.
She changes the seasons, so our crops are well fed,
And alters the colours, on the trees above our heads.
She brings to us the springtime, with life all anew,
She brings to us the summer, with skies of azure blue,
She brings to us the autumn, with its glorious reds and browns,
And finally she brings winter, when snowflakes cover the ground.
Every day she provides for us, each year her cycle is the same,
That is why this tribute is to Mother Nature,
Who brings us the sun, the wind and the rain.

Clare Allen

INSPIRATION THROUGH SONG

She was strong and determined right from the start
She knew how to sing straight from the heart
As the years passed by in the limelight she'd grow
And she'd learn how to stop the tears mid flow
Her tone and pitch both finely boned
Her skin now smooth, cheeks finely honed
Her love is that of a fairy tale
Her manager and angel, her only male
Her dedication should inspire others
To make both proud fathers and mothers
The one I speak of is Celine Dion
May her music continue when she's long gone.

Trudi James

CHILD OF NEPAL

Little in this world she owns,
Her smile was oh so sweet,
I pray that God will enable me
Put shoes on her brown bare feet.

Radiance shone on her sun-kissed face,
Twinkle in her eye,
Skipping around and having fun,
In the dense heat from a Nepal sky.

Perhaps we'll never meet again,
Though my prayers will always be,
I may see shoes on the brown bare feet,
Of that child who befriended me.

Supplies almost exhausted,
Feet swollen from the heat,
Maybe someday I'll return again,
To see shoes on her little bare feet
Of Nepalese child so sweet.

On reaching the shanty village,
Soup was prepared.
It contained four goats' feet,
Boiled with a small handful of rice
Thanking God for being sustained,
Yet again, and overwhelmed by people willing
To share their limited supplies.

In an almost forgotten country,
May God bless the feet of those who travel
The rugged mountains to help these people of Nepal.

Frances Gibson

ONCE AND FUTURE FRIENDS

It's not just simply a question of beauty, it's not a dream
For even though it's seldom we meet
I still know that if I cry alone
Or scream in whispers, you will still hear
In every single thing I do you're there
A part of me is you, a part of me is you

Far away but never distant
Out of reach but not remote
You never fail to understand my feelings, even when I can't
describe them
Your open arms are always comforting when peace is hard to find
You give and take without an obligation
You let me make mistakes and change my mind
At the times of greatest need you're there - my once and future
friends

Your seeds are sown in my heart and your music still fills my mind
Your flame burns warm and bright in my soul
And at each new corner when I turn
I find your mem'ries light the way
In every single thing I do, or say
A part of me is you, a part of me is you

Far away but never distant
Out of reach but not remote
You never fail to understand my feelings, even when I can't
describe them
Your open arms are always comforting when peace is hard to find
You give and take without an obligation
You let me make mistakes and change my mind
At the times of greatest need you're there - my once and future
friends

Never undervalue your achievements
Always seek the best in every day
Accept the hands that reach out in the darkness
And build on stones that never fade away

David Gasking

MENSTRIE VILLAGE

I stand beside the village green
Not one familiar face I've seen
I'm a stranger now for the years have flown
No one speaks I stand alone
Here in this village where I was born
I linger for a while forlorn
So many changes time has brought
Most of which was never sought
The old mill bridge where I used to play
And splash in the burn on a hot summer's day
The romantic smell of the bluebell wood
Brought memories of my childhood
I lent upon the old park gate
Strangely sad as I contemplate
No thrashing machines they're all in the past
Oh why does nothing ever last
This mining village has lost its charm
Gone are the miners, gone is the farm
Though man wasn't born to work below
Deprived of the sun and its radiant glow
Well life moves on as time goes by
So I leave my village with a pensive sigh
I make for home, my heart is cold
Time has passed and I've grown old

Euphemia McKillop

A Tribute To My Mother

Thank you for being there for me
Whenever I've needed you,
At times when there was a problem
You knew exactly what to do.
Offering a shoulder to cry on
And so many tears I've cried,
Whenever I need a cuddle
Your arms were open wide.
Sadly, no longer here in person
Now residing with the Lord,
For many years hard work
You receive his highest award.
A special place at his side
Up there in Heaven above,
Surrounded for eternity
With His gracious love.
When you were here on Earth
You always had love to give,
And I will treasure those memories
For as long as I live.

Janet Hughes

Pantoum For Milly And Cyril

The two lovers lay breathless side by side
As dawn slashed the sky and tore them apart
To live and die as one was their desire
But love letters strengthened each steadfast heart.

As dawn slashed the sky and tore them apart
Malicious time stole her hero away
But love letters strengthened each steadfast heart
And they would be together one fine day.

Malicious time stole her hero away
'Till death do us part' was but a token
And they would be together one fine day
Eyes wide open, goodbyes yet unspoken.

'Till death do us part' was but a token
To live and die as one was their desire
Eyes wide open, goodbyes yet unspoken
The two lovers lay breathless side by side.

Alma Harris

THANK YOU

To those Brylcreem Boys in Royal blue
Wings so proud and polished too
To those men who chased amongst the clouds
And wore the heavens as their shroud
To those frightened souls who stormed the beach
Firing redemption from the breach
To the jolly tars in Navy whites
Who clung to life in oily nights
To Woodbined faces on the field
Smiling for the Pathe reel
To those who scorched in desert sands
And drove the fox from foreign lands
To those who age with dignity
Who gave their youth and friends for me
To those now taken by the earth
I pray that you have found rebirth
To all who served among the ranks
My deep, sincere, eternal thanks.

Terry Cutting

MR BUTLER

I am the product of a few words,
spoken long ago in an English class.
Simple words spoken to a captive audience,
words I have remembered as the years pass.
They gave me the inspiration to begin,
to sit down and let my feelings flow.
With every word that I wrote,
my confidence seemed to grow.
Those simple words burned in my mind,
encouraging me through the hardest time.
When the river of thought ran dry,
and there were no words to rhyme.
'Poetry belongs to all men'. These words echoed.
Like a ghostly whisper from the past.
Now in this simple poem,
I get to thank you at last.

M A Challis

WITHOUT YOU

Stagnant the mind that challenged you
Broken the temper that fought you
Empty the arms that held you
Vacant the eyes that adored you
Silent the voice that soothed you
Wretched the heart that loves you
Withered the lips that kissed you
Lonely this life without you.

Jacqueline Bellas

OUR DAD

We felt that we were really blessed
Because our dad was quite the best,
He passed to us no gold, just gems,
Wisdom and knowledge were those gems.

He'd teach us how to train our eyes,
To spot a skylark in the skies,
He'd train our ears to hear the sound,
When the first cuckoo was around.

At bluebell time each year he'd see
The first white bell amid the sea
Of num'rous blooms, a carpet blue,
Their perfume rare, such wondrous hue.

Up in the beech wood he would show
Us all the trees he'd got to know,
Their leaves, their shape and all their names,
We'd stop awhile and play some games.

On Sunday nights we'd take a walk,
Up to the mountains, then he'd talk
Of people who had long since gone,
On whom the sun no longer shone.

When teaching us to live each day,
One at a time is what he'd say,
Plan for the worst, hope for the best,
Just take your time and do your best.

He's gone from us yet always lives,
In our thoughts and to us gives,
Inspired plans and hopes and schemes,
We hold his love and keep his dreams.

Catherine Craft

LITTLE DANCER

She says it all, the dancer,
with her hands behind her back;
with her little chin stuck forward,
with her beauty, grace - and lack.
She is set towards a future,
while at present in repose,
too wise to try to shape it,
enough, to know she chose.

Be not fooled by her countenance,
calm bought at a price.
For life has had its turmoil,
and fortune played its dice.
But note the one foot forward,
to step, if step it needs;
the quiet self-assurance,
that can follow where it leads.

You may fail to understand her,
for she keeps her counsel well.
Her inner thoughts, her own domain,
and hers to keep or tell.
But the peace you sense surrounds her,
is balance of all parts,
a completeness without ending,
where deepest wisdom starts.

Take pride, oh little dancer,
that you have come this far;
take courage, *life performer,*
that you are who you are!

Bridget Trafford

THE ACKWORTH SOLDIER

It was only a paper photo
On front cover of the Yorkshire Post,
He gazed upon the poppies red,
His memories were a host.
Sixty changing years had passed
Since the young villagers went away,
One or two in time returned,
Others no choice but stay.
No village stone memorial,
No familiar name on show,
Only a cross in a far-off field,
A gentle tear to flow.
Sixty changing years had passed,
When the village folk returned
In name, upon the local stone,
Erected as many had yearned.
Tom Leadbeater with beret and badge,
Leaned with stick to wonder.
Villagers in silence stood,
With many thoughts to ponder.
Wishes fulfilled, a memorial stone
To commemorate two great wars,
When young folk left a village
To fight a country's cause.
People had their memories
Of tragedies home and abroad.
British Legion stood with lowered flags
While prayers heavenward soared.
They stood as one to pay respect
In uniform, shoulder to shoulder
And gazing at those poppies red,
Was the ageing Ackworth soldier.

Walter Crooks

FREDDIE - WE WILL ALWAYS LOVE YOU

(A tribute to Freddie Mercury 1946-1991)

He told us of hid pain in a song,
The words come flowing out
From a bitter sweet tear.
'Too much love will kill you'
That said it all in a song
For that I will always remember
With the pain of dying from Aids.
But through his music he demonstrate
That 'The show must go on'.
So, the music continued,
His voice powered over and about the rest
Which after all those years
Still remain to be the best.
So that now we are in the 21st centenary
And the sake of all others
Please don't die the way that he did.
Freddie Mercury, we will remember you.

Sarah Anne Day

DEAR FRIENDS

Dear friends you've brought us much happiness
The words elude me, I wish to express
so why not say it in the written verse
Dear friends to us you'll always come first.

Like parents to my spouse, we'll let it be known
Because that enemy death has taken his own
You're kind, considerate, thoughtful and true
In life this can only be said of the very few!

For everything you've done, we appreciate
We'd like to tell you now - before it's too late
We *love you* more than words can say
For yesterday and tomorrow, but especially *today.*

Bernice Sharpe

DEAR MA

Flew across the waters to work and excel,
And bonded on the journey with Aubrey quite well,
Whom you later married in town, the first of its kind,
A Jamaican wedding, with Caribbean food aligned.

Blessed with four children, your ultimate pride and joy,
Ascended from poverty to comfort, which was the ploy,
A gracious mother to many, a true friend indeed,
Who pampered, fed and gave generously to those in need.

After retirement you were constantly on the move,
Aerobics, shopping, sewing or church, for the soul to be soothed,
We shared much laughter as you told stories of old,
Great teachings and examples you set, I hope to emulate and mould.

Your finest quality was to forgive the worst and be free from rage,
'It will destroy your soul and prevent you from living happily in age',
Grounded the family with moral, value and strength,
Created solutions for peace during a *heat* at whatever length.

Under your wing I was cared for and swamped with much love,
In return you reside with your great master above,
Although absent in flesh, your effervescent spirit is strong,
I thank you for being my precious *Dear Ma,* (my grandma),
for 25 years long.

Loving you eternally Dear Ma,
Michelle

GRANDMOTHER

Small, round and jovial,
A clown without paint,
Milk-white hair
Always under a net,
Laugh coarse as rye grass,
From past cigarettes,
Her scent is sweet lavender.

Soft as a new-born infant
In a fresh, fluffy shawl,
Her anger, a gentle breeze,
Never rises to a gale.
She hides her sadness
As I lock my secrets
In a five-year diary

Frugal her habits
Friendly her manner,
My grandmother.

Joyce Walker

A TREE SO BROAD AND TALL

A chestnut tree both high and wide
With branches thick and many
Stands in a small green meadow
A tree as picturesque as any

It stands alone for months on end
Just visited by sheep or cow
For shade from the burning sun
Apart from that, it's forgotten just for now

The time it comes into prominence
Is at the time of the conkers' fall
She is the tree the children love
The tree so broad and tall.

Keith Coleman

SAMANTHA'S POEM

When Samantha smiles
it fills her up!
No little crimpy smile at the corners of mouth,
no polite smile in a straight line -
but a big beam of happiness!

Today when Samantha smiles she fills me up
with joy and hugging,
and I am at home in a little girl of three
with red pyjamas and cheeks to match!

I used to wish I could smile like that -
absolutely open, not held in by reflex conversation,
or thoughts of bad teeth -
but I always stopped before it reached my eyes.

Now when I smile at David, Mary, friends,
at Sunflower purring like an engine,
or let my smile walk up the street
and into the village,
I smile a Samantha-smile.

When Samantha smiles it fills her up
and overflows into the room she's in.

Carolyn Garwes

SLAUGHTER OF THE INNOCENTS

You once beautiful creatures,
Graced our fields, from birth;
Shaped our landscape, gladdened our days.
Into your lives came an invisible foe.
A tireless, merciless, unstoppable foe.
An endless, spreading disaster.
A nightmare, with no awakening.
In your fields, an untimely, death.
Tainted grass, piled-up bodies.
A lonely journey, your last.
Hurled together, rotting, stinking flesh;
Shrouded, in articulated monsters.
Along country roads, through your green pastures.
Mourners, stunned, by the enormity;
Weep; in silent fields, empty stalls.
Better by far, the abattoir.
Death with dignity, in the fullness of life.
In your time of needs, we failed you.
Your blood, on our hands, forgive.

Irene Constantine

THANK YOU FOR BEING YOU

Thank you for being you
For being caring and loving too
I love you with all my heart
And hope that we will never part

Life has a way of throwing things at us
But as long as we have love nothing else matters
You want to share every aspect of your life with me
That is very obvious for all to see

Trust and honesty play a big part too
As does talking and laughing; so easy to do with you
Your mischievous smile lights up your radiant face
Life with you is all velvet, satin and lace

Well my love, every poem must end
Thanks for being my lover as well as my friend
But most of all
Thanks for just being you.

Jacqueline Gaffney

TO MY HUSBAND

To my husband,
I say thank you, for the
many things you do.
For the man in the street,
the neighbours around,
for my family, for me.
You were always there
for your mother, and mine.
A call from our friends
in need of a hand,
and you hop in the car
and do what you can.
We've been married four
and twenty years,
but it would take me
a lifetime, to say all
I could say, so I say
thank you my dear from us all.

Audrey Allen

A CAT OF DISTINCTION

Curled in an armchair
Ears twitching in sleep
Mice play in your dreams
Whilst you slumber so deep

With ginger fur shining
And tail slowly flicking
Claws flexing and stretching
Paws paddling and kicking

Prowling in darkness
Eyes shining and bright
Stalking through bushes
By palest moonlight

Pouncing on shadows
In leonine style
Sniffing the sweet scent
Of lawn camomile

Hiding in long grass
Butterfly gazing
Stretched out in sunshine
Languidly lazing

A whispered meow
As you jump on my knee
A purr of contentment
Just Henry and me

A cat of distinction
In all that you do
Sophisticate feline
This tribute's for you.

Kathryn Strangeway

ODE TO MY CAT

My long-haired black and white cat,
who sits on my lap for a chat,
Catches birds from the neighbour's tree
and I call her the terror of Battersea!

Her wild side comes to the fore,
as she climbs in the tree next door,
to silently wait for her prey,
for whichever poor bird comes her way.

She cried at my door as a stray,
I just couldn't turn her away.
So I named her Smudge and let her in,
and I've learnt with a cat you just can't win.

Her favourite occupation is to occupy my lap,
or use my chair for her daytime nap.
She commandeers with just one look,
Her name should be on the rent book!

She was a thin cat when she sat on my mat,
but contentment has changed all that.
Now she's more on the obese side,
Walking her territory with such pride.

She laps up affection and purrs like a jet,
the loudest purrer I've ever met.
I love her to pieces, I'll admit that,
My one time tatty, now ecstatic cat.

Margaret Cutler

BY HIS HAND

The gentle kiss of the midday sun
Awakens me at last -
As if from the deep depths of slumber!
The lazy impressions of drifting sleep
Are brushed from my eyes
As warming rays upon my face chase
Lingering cobwebs from my mind.
Imagination fired,
I seek to caress the canvas
As I welcolmingly embrace
The invigorating awareness
That envelops my languid body.

Sweet serenity infuses my entire being!
Gentle strokes upon my brow -
Senses which lay dormant
In the cold winter of hibernation
Are awakened with such intensity.
I feel alive and vibrant!
Foam-filled pockets of cotton-white
Strewn across a powder-blue sky!
I glory in the awesome wonder
Of this painted scene before me -
Such is this summer's day!

How little with my eyes I see!
How little with my senses feel -
With tear-filled eyes in awe I gasp
This wondrous beauty to behold!
With soul inspired and sight renewed,
With humble heart I now give thanks -
A lowly creature such as I
To witness such a sight as this!

For none could ever recreate,
No mortal hand could ever hope
To paint a picture such as this -
To touch the heart and soul as such!

Only a master of the art
Could e'er create such beauty rare.
With head bowed low I kneel in praise
And marvel at the Painter's hand!

Lucy Loretta Hegarty

HEMINGWAY

Throughout that life for which the bell has tolled
With rare honesty spoke you for your age.
Chaos, violent and turbulent conflict
You sought, for that evanescent truth, for
A peace which fled you in green waters as
The hollow horns scored and gored at last.

Not of the spider and the web you wrote,
But the twitchings of the fly. Justice you
Did to these but, as the age, in this web
Were caught, with nothing left but to deepen
The dark. Brave playboy of the western world,
Forcefully destroyed, in this, your last farewell,
You still do write your age's epitaph -
While you have found a clean and well-lit place?

Desmond Tarrant

In Memory Of Mr Schneider

Our Mr Schneider died:
    that's several years ago.
(He had TB, was frail,
    and was not so old, I know.)

We knew him, the first year
    he started sleeping out.
His house had been pulled down, and
    he wasn't one to shout.

He chose the dustbin hut
    to be his private room,
But the cold and damp arrived
    and made it like a tomb.

We found a landing, where
    he now could sleep indoors,
Stretch out his blanket, read,
    on the hard, but warmer floors.

He kept his few odd things
    in one large cardboard box:
A radio (for the weather),
    library books, a pair of socks.

We brought him soup and coffee,
    and came to know him well -
A courteous, peaceful gentleman
    whose humour you could tell.

He dearly loved the flowers,
    and would pick them from the park
To present to us, all smiling
    (thought to keep us in the dark).

At last he went to hospital,
  then . . . later . . . came the end.
We missed our Mr Schneider
  and we knew we'd lost a friend.

Katharine Holmstrom

IN PRAISE OF W J STOKOE, BOTANIST
(Author of the first British Grasses, Sedges & Rushes,
Observer Books)

He's out in the tides of spring as they come lapping
The grass roots he's treading the shadows.

His day's a quiet hill climbed scanning
The grasses, ready with fountain pen and book.

He crouches, careful, over the culled stem,
Taxonomy-wise but glad of the common name -

Before the sharp-eyed scholars made the lists
The child came calling sweet-grass and barley,

And folk-wisdom's in his bones. The old charm
Of children playing their shrilling notes

On the green blades informs his learning,
And the song of skylarks spilling heaven down.

He feels the warm bed of the leveret
And passes on, innocent of injustice,

Setting his footprints in the falling dew
Treading the seeds of the day's work deep.

Sleep will come easy to him at his day's end -
Softly as pollen spills on the winnowing wind.

Moyra Stewart Wyllie

A Tribute To You My Love

You gave me love
You taught me how to live and love
You showed me the way to go
You showed me who I am
You made me laugh
Where I would have once cried
You made me cry
Where I would have once showed no emotion
You are the brightness of day
And the darkness of night
You also are the stars in the night
You are the one
Whom I love and cherish so dear.

Violet Rustean

Grandson James

My grandson James is different in many ways
I'm Leeds United fan, that's all he says
Pictures, bedding, everything to match
No other team comes up to scratch
He's tall and slim, great in school
Not like the rest, who play the fool
When he leaves school, a chief he will be
Following in his dad's footsteps, full of glee
James is very bright and I know he will do right
He will make it, the future's in sight
    Good luck when you leave school
            Nana

Anne Davey

MY MUM/MY FRIEND

My mum
    Carried me for nine months
I hope I came up to expectation and was trumps

My mum
    Nursed me through my first tender years
At times because of me, Mum shed many tears

My mum
    Comforted me through my childhood ailments
And many teenage battlements.

My mum
    Listened and tenderly loved me from head to toe
When I was a child of woe.

The years roll on
Our memories have not gone.

My mum
    Taught me correction
I still ask her to lead me in the right direction.

For my mum
    I always find time to share
We joke and laugh at many a story and old photograph
We realise how we have changed from yesteryear.

For my mum
    I always try to have a strong shoulder
For her to lean on now we are both older.

Mary Wood

A PILGRIMAGE TO MAN'S BEST FRIEND

Tess was in her very own class
Dedication you can't surpass.
Intelligence in canine form
Apparent when she was born.

From no terrain would she shirk
In willingness and love of work.
Her understanding held no surprise
Within the loving deep brown eyes.

From craggy peaks up to the ben
Or gentler slopes along the glen,
Thro' bracken heather or wooded gill
A working inheritance of skill.

With every straggler in the flock
Accounted for and taken stock
When at last her work was done
She'd join the bairns having fun

In hide and seek around the fold
Or listen to fireside stories told
As a family member of the clan
We quite forgot her own life span.

It was her love and devotion
That set my own rescue in motion.
I'd slipped down a deep ravine
And lay shattered and unseen.

Now this cairn her resting place
No more errant ewes to chase.
I no longer the shepherd as planned
My crummock now a crutch in hand.

Yet here amid the mountains and sky
My sombre spirits can rise and fly,
Surveying nature's wondrous scale
Makes all my simple troubles pale.

H D Hensman

THE EVACUEE
(A tribute to the people of North Devon)

When the sea rolled in,
Long years ago,
A little girl away from home
Stood and watched
The pure white foam
Dashing in against the rocks.
From the city she came,
From bombs and fire,
To taste the peace
Of Devon's arms
They took her in
And gave her shelter
And protected her from harm.
She did not forget the tender care,
Or the happy homestead there,
And vowed that one day
When she could,
She'd go back to live, for good
It's fifty years and more
Since first she vowed
To leave the city and return,
And now at last, the promise kept,
She says her thank you,
And repays the debt.

Doreen P Damsell

In Awe Of Grandma

Awe-struck, I was held in her thrall again
But not in any scary evil way,
She was my grandma and she soothed my pain,
Making the sun shine brighter every day.

Grandma could do a thousand magic things
Making my world a warm and cosy space.
Holding me closely, she would sweetly sing
Transporting me to a beautiful place.

Where enchantment ruled the kingdom of dreams
Where the shadows were banished one by one,
Even drinking her castor oil just seemed
To vanquish monsters and the fevers gone.

Gran had an awesome touch, with gentle hands
And a silver voice from a golden land.

Valerie McKinley

Dedicated To My Dad Morris

Although you suffer now from Alzheimer's disease,
And you rely on your loved ones for all your needs
I hope you know my darling dad,
You were the best I could have had,
As you sat me on your knee, when I was little,
Teaching me how to pray, thanking God for every day.
I talk to God about you now
Wishing I could make you better somehow.

Alison-Jane Rainsford-Blount

REST IN PEACE
(The British Coal Industry)

No headstocks and no winding gear,
Just memories of a yesteryear,
The mines are closed, jobs are lost,
Its human life now counts the cost.

To the dole queue they do wend,
No longer working the gate end,
No more to earn an honest shilling,
Gone are the days of back filling.

Sweat and danger, dust and damp,
Their only light the Davy lamp,
Work has stopped at the coal face,
Allowing this is a disgrace.

No more to work by pillar and stall,
No shearer cutting a long wall,
No need to check the roof support,
Its foreign coal we now import.

The Government policy is, alas,
To produce power from oil and gas,
No matter how it is debated,
Our coal fields are now devastated.

No one can be overjoyed,
At people being left unemployed,
How long will this prospect lurk?
For all those men put out of work.

John Bradley

NO MEDALS FOR THE MOTHERS

I think about the mothers
Who brought their families through the war,
The short term one parent families
Who had never coped before
With ration books and coupons
As they struggled on their own
Wondering if their sons and husbands
Would one day return home.
Making-do and mending
Adding hems of different hues
To dresses growing rather short
When coupons were so few.
Conjuring in the kitchen
With ingenious recipes
To stretch the meagre rations
The appetites to please.
The nights spent in the shelters
Playing various games
To take those little minds off
The sound of fighter planes,
Whilst bombs dropped in towns and harbours
And searchlights scanned the skies
Poor mothers had to answer
To the frightened children's cries.
On reflection now I'm older
I look back in awe,
To mothers that dealt daily
With the adversities of war.

No medals for the mothers
But we salute you one and all.

Dilys Lloyd

IN EVERY STREET

(A tribute to good neighbours)

In every street there's someone who
we find are there to lend a hand,
a friend to take our troubles to
we find them, up and down this land.

'Can I help', they'll often say
if you're sad or need a friend,
their love will help you on your way
as you on life's journey wend.

They may not be rich, or in good health
but what they have, they'll share,
it may not be much, but it's more than wealth
because they show how much they care.

'Have a cup of tea', they'll say to you
whatever your troubles might be,
they seem to know when you are blue
for with understanding hearts they see.

What makes someone like them be kind
and helpful along life's way?
I'm sure that you will often find
'It's the love of god', they'll say.

'For as he's been a friend to me,
that love I want to give,
to anyone distressed I see
that's how I want to live.'

Lillian Derry

MADONNA - A TRIBUTE

The ultimate goddess of music,
a dynamic dancing machine,
an Italian-American incarnate,
a representation of the American dream.
A Michigan girl born and bred,
motherless at the age of five,
raised in Catholic austerity,
an inspiration for her musical life.
She swirled around a 'Lucky Star',
and celebrated with a 'Holiday',
the 'Material Girl', conquered the masses with her hits,
but controversy intervened on the way.
A first marriage proved to be a disaster,
her sexuality grew provocative and intense,
the relationship with the media was fraught with tension,
with 'Erotica', everyone thought she'd lost sense.
Madonna went into the wilderness,
in relationships varied and torrid,
the kiss and tell stories revealed 'an abominable woman',
a tribute indeed most horrid.
Finding solace she sought religion,
Judaism, meditation and yoga provided inner peace,
she was on the search for something eternal,
unconditional love and a sense of release.
A chance encounter in Central Park,
blossomed into a relationship of love,
a gift came along - a daughter Lourdes,
a blessing from heaven above.
But dissatisfaction with the US brought her UK bound,
marriage and children gave her happiness she'd been looking for,
her music and talent endures through the passage of time,
we wait in anticipation, for so much more.

Fine Buliciri

BEYOND THE SHORE

Grandfathers die sooner, not later:
Fabled waves that break beyond the beach.
We know no more than how such giants curl too soon;
How they fade so regularly, in the uniform of nature.
These powers in the world's ocean, a Poseidon in every wave,
Keep humanity rolling.

But how perverse when patriarchs die
Against the ocean's grain.
Not in sleep, in sickness or war -
The only ways I used to know.

Now I have surfed the queerest wave;
That although flowed and ebbed and raised its crest mighty tall,
Up of the ocean depths and floor,
Fell, whilst still employed in the nurturing of the seas.

The crash froze my reason, confusing an unready heart:
The wave that died on a stagnant pool -
Not a ripple did it make!
The wave, unfinished, hit a summer sea.
Stunned.
Still.
Not perceiving what had happened -
Suspended by the untimely passing.

Sometime, later, but not so soon,
The moon did see-saw the salt-stung wound,
And resumed its reassuring rhythm.

Grandfathers are the Neptune of their millennium's sea;
And the sea, later, learns their secret:
How each one many times their life,
Reached the comfort of the shore.

Nicholas Daniels

PRIDE AND SORROW
(To Daddy with love)

You'll never read this poem so I'll say it out aloud
And hope that you can hear me as you float upon your cloud.
There are so many things I wish that I had said,
I'm thankful for the life because of you I've led.
For the discipline and love you showed me as I grew
For the answers to the questions I ever asked you knew
For the special smile you gave me on my perfect wedding day
For the pride and sadness in your face as you gave me away.
I loved it when for weekends you'd come and stay with us
And tell my children stories and show them lots of fuss.
I'm grateful for the holidays with you that we have shared
And thankful for the many ways that you've shown us you cared.
I hope that you can hear me as I read aloud to you
I'm so proud to be your daughter and will be my whole life through.

Melanie Elphick

MY SPECIAL FRIEND

Thank you for being you
Interested in the things I do
For cheering me when I am sad
Happy for me when I am glad
For never offering advice unasked
Always ready to share a task
We have been friends for twenty years
Shared lots of laughter and some tears
I know that till the end I can depend
That you will be my very special friend.

Dorothy Richards

To The Morning

You ask
'What am I for?'
You are for me
a lighthouse
in a rocky, stormy sea
rising up straight and strong and true
no matter how
the cruel waves
batter you.
And so for me
you are a light,
guiding my awesome journey through the night
and knowing that no wind can dim your spark
you lead me to the morning through the dark.

Janna Eliot

Ode To A Hamster

A bundle of fur, all golden brown,
Rushing and tumbling, just like a clown.
A twitchy pink nose, such cute little feet,
Our dear little hamster, was ever so sweet.
Hand over hand on the bars he would go,
Ever so fast, and then very slow.
Then onto his wheel and oh what a din,
As he's running and pushing to make the wheel spin.
But one day we found him, he'd fallen asleep,
So goodbye dear Ollie - your memory we'll keep.

Margaret Whitton

FROM THE HEART

(A tribute to a true friend)

I know my mum now did me proud
Brought me through the darkest cloud
Struggled through those troubled years
When sounds of war rang in our ears
She weaned me to be proud and strong
To face the world where I belong
I know some things may have looked bad
When I was just a growing lad
Now I praise my greatest tutor
From her silver cup
Poured my golden future
All the wisdom she unfolded
Cast aside the times she scolded
All the love poured from her heart
Gave my life that special start
She taught me all I need to know
To live my life and make it glow
I thank her now with kind regards
As I face the world
Seeking its rewards

B Wardle

ANGEL WITHOUT WINGS

This is for a very special man,
who took care of me, when I was so ill,
nothing ever went to plan,
running around, to be sure I'd take my pill.

He never once thought of himself,
never had time, I was so ill,
no help outside, no one really cared,
but for him, my life was spared.

This is my tribute to that man,
so kind and warm, so gentle and sweet,
just wish sometimes, I could have done more,
this man should have a medal, my hero.

He gave me wisdom, helped me to learn,
when most days, my stomach would churn,
but now, it's my turn just to say,
give this tribute to, my man.

Julie Dawe

PUNDA MARIA
(Dedicated to my family and friends)

An area in South Africa, just above Pietersburg. Up in the mountains, where the plantations provide our world with wood.

Scattered houses, where farmers work hard, a family community, supporting each other in times of good and bad.

Sunshine fills their days despite the troubles landed on them. The whistle of trees in the wind and the falling of running water down the mountain.

Peace, calm and tranquillity fill each moment. Birds singing in the treetops, while the chattering of baboons fill the air.

Greetings and talk in local dialect, sweep across the land. Creating a humble atmosphere, where local knowledge can be obtained of times passed.

A sense of security is obtained despite the explosion of shot guns mingling with the smell of death.

It is a world of its own, no other civilisation in sight. When I see Punda Maria, I see the welcoming smiles of my dear family and friends - my ideal home.

Bridget Drinkwater

A FOREIGN GRAVE

A sleep surpassed by booming guns
We wake all huddled, men and sons
Decapitation all around
No escape that booming sound
Yet dawn is breaking overhead
Again today your workmates dead

A boom and whistling up above
More mustard gas is sent 'Mitt Luv'
So grey and lifeless is this dawn
Yellow clouds approach and spawn
Gas masks on and best be quick
Before the clouds can make you sick

Blinded 'Tommy's' now eyesight gone
More lie choking 'Quick lads run'
Damn this war, this horror show
Just to watch your mates die slow
Brigadiers and generals too
Don't care about the likes of you!

Whistle blows, barrage begins
But count the cost it takes 'Who wins'?
Nearly four years down the line
'Bang' There goes another mine!
Surgeons sewing through the night
Not indeed a pretty sight

Scarred and tattered, ripped to shreds
More tonight won't see their beds
Disease and dysentery running rife
Freezing cold, 'Cor! What a life'
Fight for King and country too
What more can they expect of you?

Give up your life, your future gone
Husband, father, brother, son!
Can't begin to know their pain
A piece of mud, a yard to gain
But what of you who look back now?
Surely they deserve a bow

Too young to know, from books we're told
Of men so brave and so bold
So spare a thought for those who gave
Rewarded with a foreign grave!

Neal Wright

GONE BUT NOT FORGOTTEN

Once there was a Princess
Who was with us for a while;
Everyone who met her
Was uplifted by her smile;
With so much love within her heart
She'd go many a country mile
To seek out those less fortunate,
To help those whose lives were grey,
But, she who had so much to give -
Her love was thrown away:
And, when she died the dreadful acts
Have never been explained
And those by whom she was betrayed
Said little and remained.
But I am sure there is a place
Where she now reigns supreme.
She was too good to prosper here
But we still can share her dream.

Leo Taylor

A POEM DEDICATED TO MRS ELEANOR ASHTON

My dear Eleanor
You are my first friend in this country three years ago
Your kindness, love and care stand by me always
Keep me warm, healthy, strong and fresh
To go through ups and downs in real life

You read my work at the first hand
You are my English personal tutor
You are always encouraging
Even though my poem is just some silly thought

When I was thirty-seven
You were seventy-three
Your birthday is the same as my nephew, Kelvin
Your daughter's birthday is the same as my brother, Kenneth
Your husband died in April
And my middle brother, Kam-ming, lost his life in the same month
What a coincidence!

What else?
Only if your son, Paul, still alive
I would have fallen in love with him
I'm attracted to him
Just by his picture
A soft heart under a gentle face.

To give and to take
We bring blessings to each other
My mother has passed away for so many years
And you have given me
The chance to celebrate
The Mothering Sunday again
You are my living mum indeed.

Mei Yuk Wong

I LOVE YOU...

I love you Caroline
From head to toe
It's taken me some time
To realise this . . . you know

I have never felt like this before
It's a constant knife's edge feeling
Like I'm breaking the law

I love the way you are so sensitive
So caring and kind
A real gem of a lady
An amazing find
I know that you love to dissect a word
And sometimes the conclusion is downright absurd!
A compliment or noble gesture
Can be misinterpreted and cause displeasure
No harm is ever intended
But unintentionally I seem to have offended.

I love the way you over analyse what I say
From the beginning
To the end of every day

I love the way I don't sleep too well at night
Because you're on my mind
And I want to hold you tight . . .

I love you Caroline.

Tim Saunders

To The Mums

I would like to pay a tribute to the mums of kids on drugs.
Once innocent sweet children, their companions now are thugs.
Their savings from a paper round, birthdays and the like
In one fell swoop was gone, just as the Christmas bike
To buy the drugs so needed, or they thought so at the time,
Whatever they could steal from home, for the pushers down the line.
Anything not locked away or stuck down in its place
They stole to sell, the habit ruled, an everlasting race.
These mums of sons and daughters have seen despair and grief
For what was once a loving child, is now a hardened thief.
Only a mother can forgive and find patience to guide
A child to get help needed, her heartbreak deep inside.
Counselling, treatment, all of them tried
Always supporting and cheerful, but when alone, she cried.
It took some years of diligence, tact, and all the guile
To wean the youngster off the drugs, a struggle but worthwhile.
Now the problem is resolved and life near normal now
Forgiven not forgotten, life must carry on somehow.
They pray the nightmare's over, the family has to thank their mum,
The child still in the circle, the lesson learnt and done.

Patricia Evans

Hesta May

She didn't have a halo
For going from place to place
She liked her home and garden,
And she had a pleasing grace.

Joining in with this and that
To her, wouldn't add any spice,
For her, her home and family
Were her 'soul' object in life.

She liked her home and garden
As wife and mother she passed the test,
And the halo she's now wearing
Is for doing her very best.

Phyllis Ludgate

TRIBUTE TO A FRIEND

I had a friend, a real good friend,
A man that everyone knew,
He was a man like most other men,
And he liked to be called Blue.

He certainly was no Richard Gere,
And mastermind was out,
But if you ever needed help,
That man was always about.

He loved a pint and a game of darts,
Of that there is no doubt,
And when it came to 'Time gentlemen please',
He was always the last man out.

His heart was as big as a house,
As anyone could see,
He was a very loyal friend,
Especially to me.

There's one more thing I'd like to say,
Round about this time,
I wish that he was here with me,
That good old friend of mine.

See you soon pal.

Roy Beaman

SABA MY FRIEND

Saba, my true and trusted friend,
for thirteen years we hiked the moors
whatever the weather,
often we would walk the roads
you and me together.

Never a cross word spoken,
nor ever a promise broken,
now the time has come my pet,
after all this time, a decision I
have to make, that will surely
break my heart.

A decision that will haunt
me for the rest of my life -
how can I decide for how long
you should live or die.
You've been such a faithful
pal of mine.

When the time came,
we sat on the floor and
held you in my arms,
you looked up at me
so trustingly
as my tears flowed
slowly.

It's hard to believe
that in a blink of an eye,
the vet had done his duty.
All I have left is a broken
heart and memories
of a faithful friend of mine.

Goodbye my beloved pet,
the angels have found
a true friend.

Kath Gabbitas

No Amount Of Years Can Stop Me Remembering

I worship you, my dearest friend
For you alone, I did so adore
Why is love only for a while on lend
All that's good, in your deep eyes I saw
My mother so sweet I miss you my dear
You're in my thoughts, in sleep and in my waking
Missing your lovely face, makes me feel fear
God took you away, and my heart is breaking
Mom, why do we live, only one day to die
All your passions gone, never again to burn
I'll never know your like again, how much I cry
Feeling my arms about you, your sweet return
How cruel to give love such as yours
Then steal you away and forever close the doors.
I miss you so, smiley face.

Ann Hathaway

MOM'S PASSING OVER

A flower snatched from our lives,
A rose plucked from our hearts,
A missing link in the family chain,
The will to live, the fight to remain here gone, exhausted.

As you drifted away, you spoke,
No one knows what was said,
But all knew for whom it was meant.

One last word of love perhaps after all those years?
One last phrase of comfort to the one who shared your tears?
One last chance of togetherness for you to share your fears?
One last breath then you were gone.

But even so you linger on,
For you are part of us, and us of you.

Sometimes things are said,
A word, a saying, a nursery rhyme,
That triggers a memory in my mind,
And I think of you.

Sometimes my mind's eye is so clear,
That I can feel your presence near,
And occasionally shed a tear, or two.

But generations must move on,
So rest in peace your time is done,
And wait for us to follow on
God bless dearest Mom.

Trevor Bruckshaw

TO A GOOD NEIGHBOUR

I'd like to say a thank you
To my neighbour Jean next door,
When my husband was in hospital
And I'd lost my dearest friend,
My beautiful golden labrador,
Had come to journey's end.

The tears I shed were many,
I felt like giving up,
My neighbour came and sat with me,
And shared the bitter cup.
She talked to me of happier days
And said they'd come again.
My eyes were red with weeping
My heart so full of pain.

Till gradually the pain did ease
I learned to cope again.
But what a blessing to me then.
Someone to share the pain
To help me through the darkest hours
Till hope had dawned again.

I've got a wonderful family,
They never forget to phone
And when their work allows it
They gather here at home,
They're the best and loving family
You'd meet on any shore,
But when life strikes that sudden blow
It's Jean who lives next door.

Isobel Laffin

JASMIN

(With love from Nanny)

On the 9th April 2001
That was the day that your life begun

I'm going to be honest, it was rather a shock
To be told you had Down's Syndrome gave us a knock

What did it mean? We knew nothing of this
I leaned into your cot and gave you a kiss

Daddy was quiet whilst Mummy shed tears
We could see in their faces the worry and fear

Through open heart surgery you put up a fight
And now we can see Jasmin, you're such a delight

With a smile like a sunbeam that lights up a room
You've stolen our hearts, there is no more gloom

Whatever the future may hold for you dear
There's one thing that's certain, your family's here

Gail Hughes

PEAKIRK - OLD PEOPLE'S OUTING

Sun on the willows and wind on the water
Rushing across at us, fading again
Mouths hard and bitter grow softer with laughter
Joys long forgotten re-surface again.

Calls of the wildfowl, flashes of colour
So different from their monotonous scene
Sitting and looking, the old and the older,
Suddenly, now, there's new life to be seen.

A voice speaks with pleasure, another will answer,
Memories of youth, and of families emerge,
Outings, disasters, all are remembered,
Suddenly life is a hymn, not a dirge

That each may feel nearer to loved ones departed,
The strength of a husband, the warmth of a wife,
Thank you, dear Lord, for the peace of the water,
The healing of sunshine, the memories of life.

Christal Medcalf

AGNES

She was Agnes,
A widow alone
In the hospice,
Quietly resigned to death,
Silently conquering her fears;
A lonely adopted child
Of seventy years ago;
Now she liked to read,
Not books with tears,
Stories she said
Where everybody lived
Happily ever after;
The nurses were dears,
But she missed her Ted,
No longer did friends visit,
Ted and they were dead;
God now surely hears
And projects
The happy ending
She has sought.

Eric Allday

THE DAMBUSTERS: A TRIBUTE TO GUY GIBSON VC

Enemy coast ahead, Germany here we come, possibly to die,
remember us, our loved ones, do not weep or ask us why,
we, 617 Squadron, came from RAF Scampton on May 16th 1943,
sending 1300 souls into oblivion, to set others free,
from Hampdens to Lancasters, this war continues without end,
this new 'Upkeep' weapon, the 5-ton bouncing bomb, we send,
to skip across water to blow apart our target dams now,
will the bomb work? Could it ever work, if so then how?
This raid is codenamed 'Chastise', that's what we'll do,
we must stop the march of the Nazi evil, another war anew,
Mother England now so far behind our imperilled tails,
through the enemy night sky the Lancaster wings sail,
hydraulic motors spin the bombs at 500rpm, to drop as we pass,
boom! Gone is the Moehne Dam, breached and losing water fast,
Barnes Wallis invented this cylindrical bouncing bomb with care,
another boom, and the Eden Dam is no more, a waterfall in the air,
some of our squadron fall from the sky, to an unknown grave,
all the German flak here is bad, can we return home, saved?
Will we ever make it home? Will we be one of the lucky few?
My God, we're going to die, we're going to . . .

Christopher Higgins

GUARDIANS OF THE FARMYARD

The sleepy farmyard started awake,
At the first cackle
Something was amiss, something wrong
The sentinels sensed it.

The perfect watchdogs, fearless and bold
Attuned to every whisper
Each stealthy footfall on grass or mud
Each breath of man or beast.

Watchmen guarding, so the farm can sleep
Feel safe that all is well
Their powerful wings could break a leg
Their hissing still a heart.

Nature's guardians, the elite force
SAS of the yard
Foxy slunk off, his tail between his legs
Farmyard peace reigned once more.

Dora Watkins

MY HERO

Once when I was five years old, I went to Barnet Fair.
    The year was 1939 and Eric took me there.
As I recall he was nineteen, my childhood hero he,
    But then a shadow crossed our world and Eric went to sea.
I'll not forget my mother's face when word arrived to say,
    Young Eric won't be coming home: 'Killed on the Jervis Bay.'
I knew not the significance - too young indeed to cry.
    It's only now in later years I've stopped and wondered, why?
It seems the Jervis Bay was sent to guard a merchant fleet,
    A convoy nearly forty strong, a hopeless task to meet.
It's known now that the captain of the valiant Jervis Bay,
    Steered straight into the firing line while the convoy made away.
So many fine young fellows slain on that November night,
    Four hours it took to sink their ship by a foe who deemed it right.
But thirty-three good ships were saved by the courage of the few,
    My Eric was just one to die with this heroic crew.
Now if you go to Chatham you can see his name in stone,
    With many others from that ship, my heroes, every one.

Gwen Farmer

TALKING ABOUT MILLIE
Eulogy on Matilda Threshie

Oh, yes, I knew Millie:
So small you'd hardly see her 'til
Those hazel eyes flashed out and shone
Like sunshine stumbled on within dark woods;
And then her nut-brown face would split apart
To spill the seeds of laughter.

Oh, yes, she took root in me!
A tiny tree but full of sap and pith,
Firmly planted in a quiet spot and
Standing straight through every climate change:
A steady shelter and familiar face
To travellers on the common path,
All walking dust together.

Oh, yes, the *tallest* tree might fall . . .
And then you'd look and solely see
A greater gap than ever there'd been tree;
The earth itself seems axe-hewn to infinity.
But quiet, buried underneath our soles
Might lie the smallest living nut,
Again to grow. *You* know.
Oh yes! *I* know Millie!

W J Dady

MRS PAJAK

Thanks Miss for all your help
Through the years we've known
The knowledge you have given me
I can now face the world on my own

Thanks again three cheers please
Keep smiling and don't shed a tear
If you don't cry I won't cry
Don't worry I'll be back next year

Jamie Barnes

MEMORIES OF FATHER

You stood so tall and so
much fun
From your seed my life began
As children we sat upon
your knee
To hear nursery rhymes
of piglets three.

It is hard to believe you are
now at rest
You were so full of life
so much zest.
We were always fascinated
always enthralled
With your childhood memories
you often recalled.

I realise how we were so
much blessed
With a father like you
a treasure, the best.
If only everyone could
have fathers too
With the kindness and caring
we had from you.

J Wood

TRIBUTE TO YOU

You don't need to leave a little light on
No I don't get any fright from the dark
When I'm with you
For when I wake up meeting the world
Well I know I'll wake up greeting you girl
In my arms
With all of your charms

(Chorus)
So don't fall asleep tonight
Not without holding me tight
And tell me when I call out your name
You'll be there
Feeling safe where
Ever you are
Mad about you when you're close to me in my arms
(Repeat)
Well I'm warm when it's cold
Only when it's you I hold
And I confront the night
For you make me sleep when I'm uptight
For when I wake meeting the world,
I know I'll wake up greeting you girl
In my arms
With all of your charms

So don't fall asleep tonight
Not without holding me tight
And tell me when I call out your name
You'll be there
Feeling safe where
Ever you are
Mad about you when you're close in my arms

Oh what's this fortune
That's beset me
Well I'm dreaming
I feel so free
When I'm with you
With all the things that you do
For when I wake meeting the world
I now I'll wake up greeting you girl
In my arms

With all your charms

So don't fall asleep tonight
Not without holding me tight
And tell me when
I call out your name
You'll be there
Feeling safe where
Ever you are
Mad about you when you're close to me in my arms
(Repeat)

No you don't need to leave a little light on.

Darren Morgan

ASSISI SET ON A HILL

So this is where St Francis dwelt
Amidst the animals and birds
The soil dry beneath his sandalled feet
The scorching sun, browned his skin and robe.
The olive trees for shade among the rocks
And distant views his eyes would see
Towards the toe of Italy.

Joan Boswell

My Mum

My mum is great,
She isn't just a mother,
Yeh, she does the mothering things,
Worries and cares about me,
Calls to check up on me,
Even though I'm all grown up and left home,
It's 'cause she loves me!

My mum is one of my best friends,
Sharing the tears and the laughs,
Always there for each other whenever,
Talking subjects have no boundaries.

My mum is so young at heart,
She's going through her second childhood,
Enjoying life to its fullest.
Just like a big kid,
Always larking around.
She's so much fun to be with,
Her joy for life spills over,
And you can't help but feel happy yourself.

Kim Rands

Mac

I shall miss you, Mac
From my daily round,
Your cheerful smile
Your kindly words.

Your lively chat
As we go in the car,
Your loyal attendance
Each week to the choir.

If your help was requested
You could never say no,
Your life was a pattern
We could all try to follow.

So at last you may rest
From your earthly chores,
May you have your reward
On those heavenly shores.

Mavis

DAD

I'll never forget our last hug, your last wave,
Though years have drifted by,
The lines round your eyes when I made you smile
Or the days I saw you cry.

Your devotion to us so plain to see
And your pride when we'd succeed,
Kind strong hands which guided us
In every hour of need.

The cold horror that filled me
When they told me that you'd died,
The cornerstone of our family
On whom we all relied.

I miss our chats and confidences,
Our hugs and walks together,
And how can I show you the thanks I feel?
But you'll live in my heart forever.

For what you left within us
Gives us power to carry on,
Your legacy of love lives there
Even though you've gone.

Catherine Champion

TOCKY

All his life he has been here
Yet we cannot predict his routine.
He knows ours well enough:
Rising at six, we blear through breakfast
And try to resist looking into the garden
For if eye-contact is made, he has won.
In he strides on rangy legs, but
Like all cats, he pleads to come in
He pleads to go out. He makes the rules.

The rest of the day is his,
He leaves no word of his route.
He may roam, he may hunt, he may charm
Affection from others. We do not know.
He is the one with the secret life.
We are transparent, easily won.
Dozing now, his eyes paw-hidden,
Like all cats, asleep in a second
Alert in a second. And flexing his claws.

Madeline Smith

THANK YOU NICOLE

Nicole, my first little granddaughter, so special to me,
Oh the joy to be had just holding her on my knee.
Such a dear little girl as bright as a button as cute as can be,
Taking such an interest all around her, so plain to see.

She came into my life after the loss of my son,
After such sadness just bringing me so much fun.
The first time I saw her she took my breath away,
She looked like him, I just didn't know what to say.

I've watched her grow with some of his ways,
In the things she does and the games she plays.
I can't describe the love in my heart that I feel,
The joy she brings when into my life the sadness steals.

Heaven-sent she was I'm as sure as can be,
She's brought so much love and joy to her family.
I just want to say thank you to her today,
May she know my love for her forever will stay.

Barbara Ann Barker

HELP THROUGH THE YEARS

When he was a baby, we kept him safe and warm,
We loved this tiny baby, even before he was born.
As the months passed by, we helped him to walk,
And as he progressed, we helped him to talk.
On life's pathway we helped him along,
Helped to teach him right from wrong.
From boy to man we watched him grow,
What was Paul's future, we didn't know.
We helped him overcome sad, bad times,
But now for our son, we sadly pine.
Our very last deed was to help Paul die,
We stayed by his bedside and said our goodbyes.
We were there with him, to the very end,
Our hearts were broken and will never mend.
                    Love you Paul,
                            from Mum and Dad.

Z Cole

THE LEGACY

I knew a man who lived so true
To what he believed, everyone knew
If he gave his word it would be done,
Though the task be hardly won.

He dearly loved his fellow-man,
His lifestyle followed a single plan,
To copy his Master was his creed,
No other incentive did he need.

His family secure within his love,
They lived a life this world above,
All those who visited their home
Never again could feel alone.

As I grew up, I came to see,
My father was my god to me,
And though the way I had been shown,
I longed for a faith that was my own!

He died: I learned to bear my cross,
Then - revelation out of loss,
Now misty eyes can clearly see
The richness of his legacy.

Olive Miller

PETER

Peter left this world today
In the very early morn
He very quietly slipped away
On this winter's dawn

Peter left this world today
He'd spent some time in pain
And through this very sad event
He'll never hurt again

Peter was a kind man
A loyal faithful friend
He thought of other people
And did so to the end

Peter left his loved ones
Who mourn his passing now
And they will sorely miss him
As only they know how

Peter left this world today
He very sadly died
I doubt there's none who knew him
Who hasn't quietly cried

Ray Ryan

BRAVEHEART

The greatest Scottish warrior that ever lived
He had one true love
The King's men killed her
He held her hankie close to his heart
As he led his men to battle
The sound of swords clashing
Could be heard miles away
The men with tartan kilts and buttocks bare
The glens were red with blood
The Princess warned him of the King's dirty deeds
Her love blossomed for him
And they kissed
And they said goodbye
For they knew their love could never be
But the seeds of love were sown
And she carried new life within her womb
The battles in the glens were brave
And the King's men captured Braveheart
And sent him to the gallows
And he shouted for freedom to the end
And the tears the Princess shed will last forever
And new life began
And her heart was full of love
For her newborn warrior

Sylvia Morrow

TRUE LOVE

We met by chance so long ago
when youth and time seemed forever.
Our love has grown stronger as the
years have passed
and we've made our life together.
Sad days and glad days we've had
them all
But our love has kept on growing
with the blessing of children to
add to our joys.
A well planned family - two girls
and two boys.

Their childhood has gone.
They're now full grown and have
little children of their own.
So the circle of life has turned
full round.
We are still so close, with a love
that's sound,
As together we face the years ahead
with companionship warm and true.
I thank God for your love
so freely given
and my joy in loving you.

Cynthia Shum

THE QUIET SERVERS

To those who serve in a quiet way,
Spreading Christ's message day by day,
In what they do, or in what they say,
At home, at school, at work or play.

It could be just a word or two,
Some little act that they do,
May be in a crowd or a few.
So why not let that one be you.

It may not be noticed what they do,
This power is God's gift to quite a few,
A chat in the train, in the bus, in the queue,
Or showing friendship, constant and true.

That friendship could mean a lot,
To an adult or a tiny tot,
Troubles that could be forgot,
Help with a surprise, they want to plot.

Just look around you, who do you see?
Ordinary folk like you and me,
So start quietly serving, then you will be,
One of the many that Christ has set free.

Will A Tilyard

MY TRIBUTE TO THE PEOPLE

I'd like to pay a tribute,
To those who make us smile,
Those folks who like to help us
And make our lives worthwhile.
To those who meet us in the street,
'Good morning,' they would say,
Just two ordinary little words
To pass the time of day.
I met a man just recently,
When tired and beginning to lag,
'My word you do look jiggered,
Just give me your heavy bag.'
'Just call at my house when coming back,'
A neighbour once called to me,
'We'll have a little natter,
I'll make us a cup of tea.'
'A trouble shared is a trouble halved,'
A dear friend one time said,
'Just spill the beans and remember,
You are quite a long time dead.'
Some people might be sceptic,
'It's only a little thing' they say,
But they are little things that mean a lot,
They make the sky less grey.
So here's a tribute to happiness,
To make life even better,
Perhaps send some lonely old soul,
A very kind and welcome letter.

Edith Antrobus

MY DAD

I remember when I was small
A daddy's girl was I,
He always made me happy
Never liked to see me cry.

We often went on picnics
Or out in the car for a run,
We'd go away to the seaside
And we'd all have so much fun.

We never had much money
But I was happy with what I had,
My mum and my two brothers
And of course the greatest dad.

It was when I was eighteen
The time we had to part,
The angels took him to heaven
It really broke my heart.

He never saw me marry
Or have children of my own,
He's missed out on so many things
I wish he could come home.

So when my children ask me
About the granddad they've never seen,
I answer them quite honestly
'He was the best there's ever been.'

Heather Logan

PAUL

Did you lose your cape?
You're my hero! You're my saviour!
You've done me a massive favour
You make me cups of tea
You let me sit upon your knee
You like to stroke my hair
You tell me that you care.

Did you mislay your horse?
You're my knight in shining armour
You always make me feel much calmer
You give me hugs and hold me tight
Snuggle up to me at night
Always praise my thoughts and ideas
Wipe away any snot with tears.

Did you run out of X-ray vision?
When you look at me I melt
You make me feel like I've never felt
You smile and it makes me smile
You put up with my 'monthlys' when I'm vile
You kiss my face and hold my hand
You do your best to understand.

You're just 'Paul' at the end of the day
I wouldn't have it any other way.

Hannah Mew

THE LOST FOREST

To walk through a forest
And behold its beauty
An ageless serenity
That mankind enjoys

Now cut down and burnt
No life nor breath
Seeds of ashen wood
Speak forth of death

No singing wind
Across the canopy
Of leaves and branches
That once sang here

The beauty of this place
Lost in a moment
Lost of humanity
Never to be seen again

We can save the future
If only we can see
Heal the cut in nature's side
And let the forest be free

Stand in timeless motion
As the trees sing to you
Listen to the music
And never let it go

The final choice is yours
Before it's lost in time
Let your children hear the music
Let them rejoice in its rhyme

As the trees murmur the words softly above

Colin Skilton

DIANA

She had found happiness at last
Regardless of an uncertain past
Only to be snatched away
In a car driven far too fast

It should never have happened
Some even say it was planned
The accident took her away
To a far-off land

We were stunned and shocked
A nation in mourning
The People's Princess
No longer adorning

William and Harry
Just what will they do
To replace their mother's deep love
That they always knew

We as a nation must come to terms
With losing an icon for whose love many yearn
It's hard to accept and we don't know
Why such an angel of God should have to die

Floral tributes showed how many felt
When an untimely death was cruelly dealt
Let her now rest in peace safe in the hands of God
Our maker in the promised land

Lynne Taylor

MY GRANDCHILDREN

For years I waited for the day
My grandchild would be born.
Time went by and hopes grew dim
And left me quite forlorn.
Then at last I heard the news
A child was on the way,
I thanked my Lord, my heart o'erflowed
With joy that happy day.

He has arrived, a lovely boy
With such a happy smile,
I wheel him round the leafy lanes,
He's sleeping for a while.
Then he awakes and looks around,
With trust he smiles at me,
'Tis happiness beyond compare
Which God has given free.

The years have passed, the family's grown
And he is 12 years old.
Now a brother and a sister
Have joined the happy fold.
My home is now their second home,
They come and show they care,
I thank my God that I'm so blessed,
Their childhood days to share.

Beryl R Daintree

MY SISTER, DEBS

In times of trouble
I know you'll be there
You'll be the one
To show me who cares
You'll offer advice
And support me too
It's great knowing I have
A sister like you

We live far apart
But not far in our thoughts
If I feel I'm falling
I know I'll be caught
You are the one who is there, standing by
Never asking questions like
How, what, where, why?

We're here for each other
From beginning to end
And with this poem
It's love I will send
For listening to me and
Showing you care
And to say thank you
For just being there.

Lisa Bennett

MIRACLE OF LIFE

Oh, miracle of life
I've longed for you to be
Your being here's so right
You mean the world to me
Your beauty's so remarkable
I hold your life so dear
Come snuggle in my arms
I can't believe you're here

Oh, miracle of life
So innocent, so true
A gift from heavens high
I owe so much to you
My joy is almost tangible
I celebrate your dawn
A lifetime's bond established
The moment you were born

Oh, miracle of life
You're growing by the day
You fill me with delight
With deepest thanks, I pray
You smile's so irresistible
Your laughter melts my heart
Your love is so dependable
You've had mine from the start

Oh, miracle of life
May angels steer your course
I'm always here to help you
And all I have is yours
I cherish every heartbeat
Each precious breath you draw
My miracle of life
I couldn't love you more.

John Hartley

An Ode To My Friend

What gossamer threads, though strong as steel
Bind us together - friend to friend.
What common ground do we share
In spoken and unspoken words, deeds' success,
Shared hurt, solemn occasion, or laughter's mirth.
Life is the better for the knowing.
Life the richer for the sharing.
But if future fates one day decide -
That our paths are to divide,
Then I will grieve at loss of face and form,
And hold closely to all gone before,
Treasure future contact in whatever form.
And if sometimes to tears I lend
'Twill be because I miss my friend.

Celia Parkin

For A Lady

You left with all the speed of dark
Unhindered by a last farewell.
Time passed, I stood, I looked, I listened.
Do you speak to me in birdsong
Or whisper with this sibilant wind?
Are you the green of leaf above, or grass below?
Are you the blue beyond the sky?
Is your breath the air I breathe?
Are you happy, are you sad? I'll never know.
But all of you is here - inside my head.

Rob Brown

TRIBUTE TO MY DAD - ALEXANDER MORRISON
1926-1988

He liked to sit looking out
Of the scullery window
Smoking his cigarettes,
Drinking stewed tea,
Thinking about life.
He could have been a philosopher,
Or a writer, my dad.
A big man with a gentle heart.
He says, 'There are only two things ye canna be a little bit!'
'What's that?'
'You canna be a little bit pregnant
Or a little bit dead!'
And we all laugh!

I comb his hair with the pink comb.
I don't like the Brylcreem
Sticking to my fingers.
He likes to let me comb his hair
While he has forty winks.
His hair is very grey. He says,
'It's not, it's ash blond!'
And we all laugh.

Dad's not well, they take him to hospital.
He has lung cancer, he won't get better.
He tries to cheer us up,
But we can't laugh!

He passed away, my dad,
And we thought we'd lost him forever.
But now we remember like it was yesterday,
All the funny things he did and said
And we all laugh!

Christine Nuttall

FOREVER IN MY HEART

Christine, my mother
Happy-go-lucky
Really, really super mother
Intelligent, my mother
Super mum
Tender love always
In my thoughts always
Never ever forgotten
Everlasting love I have for you
Mother, I love you
You're my mother Christine
Forever in my heart
Memories happy I have
Underneath the stars I look and think of you
Marvellous, marvellous woman
Important, intelligent, lovely woman
Love you always
Open my heart to you
Very, very important, my mum
Every day you're in my thoughts
Now sadly not with me here
Now in heaven with God
You Christine, an angel
Always and forever in my heart
Opinions of yours l liked
A super mother
Definitely love you always and forever Mum
Forever in my heart

Michelle Knight

HOME

It was a few months after she died
That her daughter hankered for home.

Not her own, but her mother's
With a wanting to stand at the soul's citadel

To see where she rose each morning to grind the millstone parched
In the heat from the garden of wheat and dry, cracked, punished soil

To hear the conversations at the water well
Of disbelieving truths that village girls told in their
                                        garments of silk and sack-cloth

To touch the baking oven where her mother taught her to cook
For a husband whose mother told him never to be weakly grateful

To know the places where her father had lost himself daily amidst
                                        the amused temper of servitude

And to know when her mother had found herself daily unable to
                                        bear the caress of fateful endings

When she died she told her daughter that she knew
That the cracked soil could never be healed, that girls dared to lie
That her father was never found out and that her mother never
                                        lived within

And she breathed in the smell of her mother's relinquishing hands
Yearning while she waited for someone to let her in

Feryad A Hussain

TO A WAR TIME FIREMAN

Sleep on, old friend, sleep on,
And wake no more to this world's stark grey dawns,
But take your timeless rest in tranquil peace.
Gone the clarion calls which brought you once
To derring-do and roaring fearsome flame;
O'ercome by your undaunted spirit bold,
Undismayed, e'en though furnaces of hell
Quick sought to scour you from this mortal coil.

Long gone your happy band of brothers brave,
Who, with you, fought the fires of evil war.
Rejoin them, arms around you, rank on rank;
Embrace again the brotherhood you earned
Through searing heat and burning, blinding brands.
Ne'er dream again those awesome nightmare scenes
Reminding you of comrades cruelly lost,
And grieving wives, who wept for their grey ghosts.

Take now your place amongst your kindred kind;
Those ordinary British working folk
Who rose to famed acclaim when needed most.
Your actions shone so bright in those dire days,
Eclipsing all you ever strived to do.
Rest now, at ease, 'mongst those with whom you served,
As now, for you, the bells go down no more.
Sleep on, old friend, sleep on.

Ron Shettle

IN PRAISE OF THE LATE THOMAS HENRY

A child of lost and long-forgotten days,
Outdated laws and antiquated ways;
A boy, a youth, a man not in his prime,
A classic illustration of his time.

But I saw him the way a child would see:
The first man in my life was old to me;
I looked on him with reverence and fear;
I could not see beneath the harsh veneer.

He disciplined himself and tutored me
In self-restraint, control and honesty.
And all his wisdom stood me in good stead,
A firm foundation for the years ahead.

And though I always looked on him in awe,
There was a gentler side I rarely saw;
A warm and kindly man who never dared
Take off the mask and show me that he cared.

At last his true emotions filtered through
As he reached twilight years, as all must do;
And as the wall around him disappeared,
The mist became less cloudy, and then cleared,

And I could see the man he'd really been,
And not the one that hitherto I'd seen;
No longer looking with an infant's eyes,
Gone was the mask and cloak, the old disguise.

And so I had a chance to really know
This man, and let my feelings for him grow;
And he allowed himself the liberty
Of candour, and professed his love for me.

So I give thanks that I was not denied
The time to know this man before he died.

Hilary J Cairns

CRUSHED VALLEY

She sits upon a graveside
She says 'Your mam is here'
She cannot hide the pain inside
She's lost all she holds dear.

More than 100 mothers
Are weeping by her side
Due to the mistakes of others
All their children have died.

The Coal Board had been tipping
The coal waste up too high
The mountain started slipping
Meaning all below would die.

Down into the valley
The mount began to slide
Engulfing a little school
With the children still inside.

After every frantic effort
So many wouldn't survive
A parent's worst nightmare
Seeing their children buried alive.

This is the painful story
Of the day a mountain fell
It sent the village of Aberfan
Into a permanent hell.

God bless the people of Aberfan
Give them peace and ease their pain
Through them may we learn a lesson
It must never happen again.

Marie Horridge

FAMILY LOVE

I must pay tribute to my daughter and son
They are both so thoughtful, loving and kind
They come anytime to our house when they can
And ask is there anything they can do at all.
My daughter I see almost every day
I go to her house, or she comes to call
When I'm feeling down, she picks me up
We have a good laugh, sometimes a frown
She confides in me, I confide in her
And sometimes the problems just fade away
So thank you Maria, for just being there
And thank you Edward, my son, for all you do
And thanks to Maureen, your wife
And Maria's husband Tony, too
And to my husband Albert, without him they would not exist
For your love, thoughtfulness and kindness too.

Margaret Stumpp

UNCLE JACK

Lonely parting has hid your heart, where this world still chills,
Rescuing fellow soldiers at Dunkirk in the medical corps,
Only family continue your soft heartbeat in grateful memories,
Heads turned in amazement, but one in war-torn Europe!
Recognised by your brother Ben,
A jewel to mellow sadness,
Circumstances may cloud, yet disappear in family love,
Evaporating like the early morning mist to reveal you,
Uncle Jack!

Martin Norman

CHRISTOPHER MARLOWE (1989)

This is about someone from the Elizabethan age,
Someone that is famous for creating entertainment on stage,
And his name is Christopher Marlowe.
His plays were superb - each one turned out to be a great show!
He was the son of a shoemaker, and his family was very poor.
Once the public saw one of Marlowe's plays, they wanted to see more.
One of the plays he wrote was called 'Tamburlaine the Great'.
William Shakespeare was his mate.
Marlowe's friends called him 'Kit',
That's a strange nickname, isn't it?
'The Massacre of Paris' was another play he wrote.
I wouldn't miss the chance to see any plays written by Marlowe.
It is believed that Marlowe died in a tavern brawl,
But I don't believe that at all.

Jason Pointing

DIANA PRINCESS OF WALES

A princess so rare
Like the sun in the sky
Spreading its rays in all directions
The love which poured from your heart
Touched all.
If the world's tears were collected
On your passing
The remembrance garden would never
need to be watered.

Catherine Torode

STRAWBERRY FIELDS

And so I went to Strawberry Fields,
A natural park of gardens, shrubs and trees,
Planned in memory of the Beatle, John Lennon.
No plants grow finer, no trees taller than these.
This autumn day no flowers are blooming
But the trees are a mass of yellow, red and gold,
And a young boy in the distance plays guitar and sings
Where the breeze blows moist and cold.
But here is a mosaic memorial to a great songwriter
Whose life was ended by an assassin's gun,
When the genius of his work was at its highest
And the healing of his tortured soul had just begun.
Yesterday the wind blew cold down Penny Lane,
A kind of sadness filled the troubled air.
Imagine a world without the Beatles' music!
Imagine a garden, shrivelled, brown and bare!
It is afternoon when I see the mosaic circle
When the autumn glow of day is beginning to fade,
And there, in its centre, stark in its loveliness
Bright on the grey stones, a single red rose is laid.
Then in the uncanny silence of Strawberry Fields,
A toddling baby picks up the rose and holds it in his hand,
And smiles, as babies always will
In innocence, for he does not understand.
But the quality of his smile has surely told
That although yesterday's genius has gone,
And will not be forgotten in this age,
Yet new songwriters wait to go on and on.
Suddenly melancholia flies upon the wind,
The baby to the stones the red rose yields
And smiling still, totters to his mother,
And like gentle mist, peace fills the air in Strawberry Fields.

Win Wilcock

MY GRANDCHILDREN

Oh what a glorious feeling
When your first grandchild is born
It's a feeling sublime
To know she's carrying on the line

You think she looks a bit like you
She's cute and very intelligent
She looks at you through eyes of blue
And you think she's heaven-sent

Then along comes your first grandson
He's a handsome lad, just like dear old dad
He's mischievous - a little imp
When he looks at you, you just go limp

Then number three grandchild is born
She's a tinker and terribly funny
She sings and she dances
She preens and she prances
She's a little honey

When your fourth grandchild is born
You find her so endearing
She's got a smile to light up the darkest night
She captured your heart, right from the start
She's a darling and so appealing

They're all adorable and yet so different
And you love them all equally
You've so much love to give to them
As they enrich your life immeasurably

Phyllis L Stark

OUR PET MAJOR

Did I ever tell you we once had a Labrador for a pet?
I also meant to tell you that it is a thing we do not regret,
The hours of fun he gave us all, the laughter that he caused
From hiding Grandpa's slippers underneath a set of drawers.
When running in the garden chasing frogs across the grass
To falling in the fishpond, what an awful splash!

When called in for his dinner he would skid across the floor
Then time to take him for a walk, he would race us to the door
He made noises from his throat trying very hard to speak
All the effort that he made and out came one big squeak.
So smart was our dog Major when we were playing games
He would muzzle in and seemed to know the children by their names.

Table tennis we were playing, he would try to catch the ball
One day he accidentally swallowed one and he was not well at all.
To the vets we rushed him with everyone concerned
The vet looked at him kindly and said
'I hope a lesson you have learned.'
We stayed all night beside him he certainly was sick
But the medicine the vet prescribed really did the trick.

He was a really tough little fellow and we all miss him so
Just like everything on this earth someday you have to go.
A real good friend was Major and no other can take his place
We only have to think of him and the tears run down our face.

Flo E Smith

HEART OF GOLD

When you were only seven
Your mother said to you
'You have a sister now to care for
See how small she is
And she only has us two.'

You have done your very best
Through the many years we've shared
And even when Mother had gone
You showed me how you cared.

You learned First Aid, helped Brownies
And cared for 'oldies' too,
Whenever help was wanted
People always came to you;

And even now that you are frail
Almost blind yourself,
Your heart of gold is shining bright
Like a lamp upon a shelf.

All the village knows you,
Shopkeepers, bus drivers too
And when you leave this life,
In Heaven where Mother waits,
She'll be very proud of you.

Deirdre White

PRECIOUS ANGELS
(Dedicated to Shannon and Lukas)

Lying here the moon still and bright
Looking around in the silent candle light

I see them in their cradles looking real sweet
Tucked beneath their tiny white sheets

They are so special, nothing can compare
To precious angels who we love and care

They are such a beautiful bundle of fun
They have made my life the happiest one

I love my children with all my heart
I swear to God we'll never be apart

If anyone hurts them they'll answer to me
As they are more special and precious than anything you see

Just like a distant special dream
Thank you, you make my life worth living

Michelle Barnes

A POEM FOR KIM

Who was it who found me deep in the dark forest
and wounded in love? Who was the one
who brought me in from the hungry storm
and ravenous rain? Who was that special someone
who lifted me up when all the others put me down?
It was you, it could only have been you.

Nigel David Evans

You Are, I Am

Your warmth,
your wisdom
are with me
forever

You changed my life
for the better
I am better
because of you.

Your humanity
touches me
from the outside
and seeps deep inside me,
inspiring me.

Your patience
teaches me
with its gentle, guiding hands.

You surround me
with your spirit,
absorb my pain
with a single, tender glance.

You are beside me,
within me
you are with me
always.

Katy Connell

TRIBUTE FOR AMANDA

Amanda coped with inner pain,
With dignity, so sweet.
She gave more love than most contain,
Showed courage in retreat.
A gentle warmth and humour
Brought light, creative flair,
No gossip, farce or rumour,
A breath of clean fresh air.
Sensitive, no vicious streak,
As trusting as a child.
She bore the pain, but did not speak,
so deep emotions piled
With force, and filled her gentle life
With more than she could bear,
So poor Amanda gave that life,
In innocence, unfair!
She did have times when anger stirred
And tears she had to cry
But rarely spoke a bitter word,
Her deep desire to try.
Criticism does not hold
But there may be reform.
Her deep distress was not consoled,
But passage through life's storm
Allows Amanda's friends to see
What true affection means,
The snare of pain has set her free
To rest behind the scenes.

Emma Louise Taylor

TO MY TWIN BROTHER

I never knew him; not in fullest life.
We shared a womb. Full time, he led the way
(The doctor said) to ease the path for me.
And so he died; and so, through him, I lived.

I have his mind, his attitude to life;
His masculine approach, his way of thinking.
If he had lived, would I still be half him,
And he half me? Or would we, being apart,
Take each our separate identities?

I never knew him; even so, I miss him;
I miss our arguments, exchange of thoughts;
I miss our walks together and our play;
I miss our school time and our college days,
Our young adulthood, shared maturity.
Would we have shared the same strong interests
In nature, travel, art, and in our work?

Which of us would have been the first to die,
And how?
                    Why ask? We know who did.
- But if -

What sort of person would he have become?

Would he have given me a single thought,
Or missed the sister he had never known?

F Jones

FANTASY OF LOVE

Dream lover, with eyes of blue
Why am I so in love with you?
Every night I go to sleep,
You come to me with love so sweet
You hold me close with loving tenderness
Why, oh why can I never make you mine?
You kiss my lips and whisper sweet nothings in my ear
Loving you like I do puts me on another planet
You give me such happiness you nearly drive me insane
I long for your touch, I long for your lips to inspire my need
I love you so very much, you satisfy my greed
Of you I can never receive enough, I need you, I miss you
My life is lonely without your arms to hold close
You gave me so much, darling, I love you
You will always share my heart.
And that's why we will never part!
Back to fantasy of love and dreams.

M S Cornbill

FOR JOHN

His life was short
But it was a song
Of music and drums
And bands and gigs.

His life was short
But it was an art
Of drawings and paintings
Sketches and oils.

His life was short
But it was full
Of all that he wanted
To do and say.

His life was short
But there was joy
And laughter and love
Now happy memories.

Marie Housam

THANK YOU

(Written on my husband's retirement earlier this year from Downham High School.)

My thanks go to you one and all
For your friendship and kindness to me.
Unfortunately I cannot go on
As you probably all can see.
I've enjoyed my time at Downham High
But the time has come to go
I will miss you all as time goes by
But the rubbish is thrown down too low
The little darlings I will miss as well
But I think they have given me hope
Hope for what I cannot tell
I can't sit around and hope.
I wish you all the best of luck
As you travel your chosen road
Let someone else have all the muck
As I've emptied my very last load.

J E Nicholls

DAVE

You like the dawn
I like the dark
You like beginning
I dread ending
You like challenge
I feel scared
You want the future
I crave the past
You enjoy today
I don't notice
Today becomes tomorrow
The present becomes the past
The future is only hoped for
The lesson you've taught me
Is to make life count!

J Campbell

FRIENDSHIP

I have a friend a really good friend
Who would do anything for me
He's there in any crisis
As he thinks the world of me
When I'm feeling very down
And instead of a smile, I wear a frown
He comes over to cheer me up
Telling jokes that fill me up
He stays with me for quite a while
To make me laugh, and make me smile
But when he leaves I smile and wave
And thank the Lord for the friendship he gave.

Diana Daley

TUCKER

(Dedicated to my sister Sylvia)

He lived next door, a neighbour yet more
He would give you sixpence for brushing his floor
With lots of praise he made your confidence soar
And you knew all your troubles to him you could pour

He had a rubbery face, but it was very kind
You knew if you made a mess, he wouldn't really mind
He put up with us all even when we argued and whined
He fed us rabbit stew and pink rice whenever we dined

When Mum and him fell out, he'd buy her 20 Park Drive
Hoping she'd accept and their friendship he could revive
He sometimes rolled his own, at least four or five
They both enjoyed smoking it made them feel alive

He bought us comics and sweets, he gave us pocket money
He made burnt potato crisps which we thought were yummy
We'd play rounders in the evening whenever it was sunny
He loved us all dearly but I think his favourite was Mummy!

He could hear the grass grow, he even knew how to sail
When in the jungle he swung an elephant round by its tail
We loved all these stories, so we'd visit him without fail
Eating Stork margarine on toast while listening to yet another tale

He didn't have any family, we were all that he had
He used to tell us stories about when he was a lad
When we sang him 'Old Shep' he would become very sad
Mummy said we were naughty that our behaviour was bad

I remember the time he chopped off Tom Dooley's head
He chased him with an axe what a dance he was led
He shouted and roared we couldn't repeat what he said
But we missed him a lot when we were told he was dead!

Maggie Fairbrace

IN SPIRIT

Come on be strong, you can make it,
I hear him say, each time another problem arrives,
Don't duck out, you've got through worse situations.
I recall so many now, they all seem to blend into one.
But nine years ago, the one that hurt the most,
Was when he suddenly left me.
No more chats, advice or laughter, no more walks across the heath,
Eating ice creams, as we did when I was a child and since.
No one to look up to, no more boats, trains and planes or swings,
What happened to all those childish things?
Yesterdays full of sweet encouragements and love,
Snatched away like a child's toy when it's been naughty.

Life goes on, perhaps it does, but so many gentle reminders flash
before my eyes,
It pains me, knowing he cannot smell the summer rose, feel the dewy
grass at dawn.
Nor watch the sunset sink beneath the skyline each night,
As a giant velvet curtain is drawn across silently.
I hear his favourite song, or see an ancient black and white movie,
I smile remembering his face full of enjoyment, I wipe away a
sneaky tear,
And so my dearest Father, it was one very early Sunday morning,
No warning, no goodbyes, that you were taken from me,
The sadness is never far, but the memories are one hundredfold,
They always return when required and in my heart you live on
and on and on . . .

Amanda-Lea Manning

THANKS

It was something I could not do,
So 'another', gave birth to you.
Your natural mother already knew,
Adoption would be best for you.
Minutes with her baby were few,
For her a nightmare had come true.
She faced the future without you,
And did what she had to do,
Although you took a different view,
When into a teenager you grew.
Sad thoughts came into your head,
When you looked at us and said,
'She never really did love me,
Or my adoption would never be.'

A grown-up yourself, now you see,
Giving baby away was a high fee.
When she gave you to Dad and me,
Never to know your baby days,
With us that memory ever stays.
Your birth to her now only a haze,
What you look like, your special ways.
A special daughter, we love you,
Our thanks to her are overdue.
Without her, we would not have you!

Sheila Walters

MY TRIBUTE

You called to me and I came
Driving through the night
I wandered through the darkness
Guided by your light
A love that has not flowered
Is the seed of eternity
And time is very long
For those who have to wait
But a life without love is no life at all
Falling tears in your bed
I find hard to explain
Perhaps confused emotions
Bring back the crying game
Souvenirs and treasures scattered all around
Memories of my yesteryears echo through the sounds
Tolkein lies abandoned deserving to be read
Tea and orange juice breakfast in bed
The day was filled with mourning
As history takes its toll
A queen, a sister, a mother
Sent a nation out of control
A once caged animal lies sleeping at my feet
A name with such command now scolded soft and sweet
I am grateful for those moments
I almost shared with you
When the future recalls the past
And asks me what I did
I will picture you in your castle
Like a candle in the wind.

Linda Doel

SAINT DAVID

Saint David is our patron saint
Some think our customs rather quaint.

He was brave and he was bold
His many exploits were not told.

He was tall and he was gaunt
Though his stature, he did not flaunt.

His expertise was there to see
Advice for all without a fee.

He did much good for one and all
Saint David heeded every call.

The place he loved is now famed
As all its predators are tamed.

Despite the ravages of tide and time
Saint David's home is in its prime.

His name lives on in his fair city
He has no equal more is the pity.

Saint David scans the murky past
Knowing full well he rests at last.

J A Harries

FOR IAIN

A few brief months you filled my life with joy
Your gentle nature kindly, true and strong;
You made me trust the wonder of your love,
Restored lost confidence, changed grief to song.

Together we laughed at pantomime jokes,
The ugly sisters in dazzling array;
Were awed by Tchaikovsky's vision of hell
Listened to Haydn and heard John Lill play.

In sunshine we sat at lovely Culzean,
Your arm around me, saw children at play;
Watched graceful swans drifting silently by,
Content to enjoy the peace of the day.

We worshipped together, prayed that our lives
Might always be lived in praise of our Lord;
I wanted your teaching - wisdom of years
Spent in His service and spreading His word.

So short a time we shared, for mourning cards
Came in the post with wedding wishes too;
But I thank God for all you showed of Him,
And for the precious gift of knowing you.

Barbara Jefferies

SECOND-HAND HEROES

They were for sale on a stall in the market
Eight discs of silver or gold.
A shame for the men who had earned them
Their story will never be told.

How grateful or wonderful nation
Felt at the end of the strife
To the men who had fought so bravely
And to those who had given their life.

They wrought these medals for valour
They were given with pomp and acclaim
The men had a 'Pass-by' and dinner
To acknowledge their right to some fame.

The world then promptly forgot them
They were left to struggle and strive
They *had* to sell their medals
In order to stay alive.

D Adams

GRANDAD M

Upright, stern, moustachio'd he,
man of utmost solemnity,
Grandad M,
deserving special mention.

Honest, fair, devotional he,
man of deepest integrity,
Grandad M,
respected, man of convention.

Serious, devout, yet cheerful he,
whistler of Strauss and hymnody,
Grandad M,
example of non-pretention.

Craftsman repairer of watches and clocks,
strong of faith: God never mocks.
Grandad M,
lived by good intention.

Long since gone to heaven, he,
but still respected in memory,
Grandad M,
still deserving mention.

Ann Voaden

A Tribute To A Curlew

From far away in the green, cool marshes
In the dusky, evening light
An eerie cry reaches my ears
Long, low
Mournful.
I have not heard a call like it in all my wanderings,
It haunts my mind,
It haunts my very being,
Mournful,
Long, low.
Cry on, cry on thou strange brown bird,
With long and curvéd beak.
Cast thy ethereal spell on all the world this night,
Again on the sweet balmy air that cry,
Long, low,
Mournful.

Vivian Khan

To The People I've Known

Oh so many people can inspire you on life's way,
You meet with different characters nearly every day.
Your life is like a melting pot, full of varied things,
Whatever stage you are in life, another taste it brings.

My grandparents and parents, I thank them from my heart,
For without their love and guidance I wouldn't have a start.
But children, friends and family are all so special too,
My husband who is always there, you know that I love you.

Our little pets we've cared for over all the years,
When they've had to leave us, I've shed so many tears.
A tribute and a thank you to the people from the past,
There have been so many I've admired, the list is all so vast.

The people I have yet to meet, is exciting just the same,
Another friend, a grandchild, to know another name.
One tribute is so hard to do, so many that I see,
For everyone I've known as yet, are all a part of me.

Thank you all.

Betty Hattersley

UPON A FAMOUS ACTOR

His moods vary as the day
Does mould itself around him,
And asking nothing of it,
He daydreams this life away.
But sometimes, he is shaken
By strong demands upon him;
And then; behold, rare beauty!
Words he speaks so meaningful,
With lips that strongly caress;
First holding each one upon them,
As though it were a living thing,
Then launching chain creations
Like slow suspended puppets
- Animated words, shaped
By his own expressing lips
From deep feeling so intense,
Passing from his spirit, to living words, to our spirit.

John M Reeve

A FRIEND

A friend is always there
When you are down, and full of despair,
You think that there is no lower to go,
And then you hear a cheerful hello.
She stops for a chat, and asks how you are,
And when she sees you are near to tears
She tells you she will always be there.
You feel so much better to know somebody cares,
And that a friend will always be there.

When I am at rock bottom, I give her a ring
Just to hear her voice makes me feel I must win.
She is never too busy to listen to me,
She says that is how a friend ought to be.

B R Boyt

STAR

You try to press your passion down
and pin it to a page,
but words like yours cry out for life,
so step to centre stage.
The scene is set, you know the script,
it's time to raise the curtain.
We'll all be out there cheering for you -
knowing you, we're certain
that when you face the world
and start to speak your opening line
you won't need any prompting
to tell you how to shine.

Stephanie Cage

MY DOG SAM

A thing of beauty is you standing there,
The sun on your back and the wind in your hair.
The love in your eyes as you wait there for me
Was stronger than mountains and deep as the sea.
I miss you so much my beautiful boy
When you were with me my life was all joy.
The walks that we shared in the fresh country air
We used to walk miles with never a care.
We discovered so much together we two
The green of the trees and the sky that was blue.
The sunsets of red, the birds that we fed.
The cold winter snow, the winds that did blow
The cool of the rain in a small country lane.
The butterflies, the flowers we gazed at for hours.
The stars and the moon, the sunshine in June.
You made me laugh with your funny ways
You made me happy even on sad days.
So many friends we made on our walks,
We always enjoyed our daily talks.
These people I would never have known if I had not made you my
very own.

I know you're still near just a whisper away
And we will be together again one happy day.
I feel you in the breeze, I see you in the trees.
Your face is on my pillow at night when I dream.
The smell of your fur so fresh and so clean.
I'll never forget you my faithful old friend
So loyal and loving right up to the end.
I know you're just a breath away listening to everything that I say.
Be happy my darling and free from life's pain.
Till we meet once more on the celestial plain, where we belong
together again.

Christina M Sturman

HOMECOMING

I had a dream the other night,
And as you know I dream a lot,
the dream I dreamt was of a man
the poet, T S Eliot.
He was sailing in a broad-beamed boat,
Running with the wind and tide,
Accompanied by his friends and folk
All standing at his side.
The boat he sat in was not of burnished gold,
But built of solid English oak.
Now you may think this man austere,
As one whose thoughts you'd have to guess,
But sailing in his boat with friends,
He radiated happiness.
A thousand boats had put to sea
To celebrate his poetry,
Bedecked with flags and finery,
They followed in his wake,
And from the shore you could hear
All the people shout and cheer.
With klaxon sounds and foghorn's blare
It was a glorious homecoming affair,
And waiting for him to drive away,
Upon the quay, a bright red Maserati.
Now why this dream should come to me
Is something of a mystery.
I know little of his biography,
As teacher, bank clerk, PhD.
I only know that unlike some,
He sailed the seas and lived a life of poetry,
And now he's home.

Stewart Gordon

DIAMONDS IN THE SKY

Worth more than gems,
I would say.
As you race across the sky
Everyone will say
I saw the *Red Arrows* today.
Your courage and skill
Remembered by all.
Young and old.
Gasp as they behold
Daring feats.

Red One to Red Nine.
Also Red Ten
Those on the ground.
Everyone
Deserves praise.
No time to think
Up there in the sky.
As you land
It is a job well done.
Applause from everyone.

A wonderful team.
The ones never seen
Who look after the planes.
Help you to fly
Up there so high.
Everyone
Will remember
Your flights in the heavens.
I will say with pride
I saw the *Red Arrows* today.

Thora Carpenter

FLOPSY'S WEDDING

(A tribute to Beatrix Potter)

Flopsy Bunny went on a spree,
Hoping someone nice to see
When little Miss Flossy came down the lane,
He looked just once and he looked again
For little Miss Flossy was small and neat
With a dear little bobtail and twinkling feet
It was love at first sight and he knew he was right
'Dear little Flossy, please marry me,'
'Gladly,' she said, ' I your bride will be.'
Padre McGreggor live down the lane
Just by the church and they made it quite plain
Would he, the Padre, perform quite soon,
'I'd be delighted, of course, my dears,
May you be happy for many years.'
A marriage for them on the 10th of June.
The Tailor of Gloucester was asked to play
The organ for them in his finest way
Squirrel Nutkin the best man they asked to be
And then came Tom Kitten with children three
Two to be bridesmaids and one a page
How exciting for them to take centre stage,
Jeremy Fisher arranged the pews
As usher to see that they had good views,
Dear Tiggywinkle, a place for you
But no one likes Prickles, be careful do
The Wedding March sounded and up the aisle
Came Nutkin with Flossy, a happy smile
Flopsy and Flossy were duly wed
'Now for the toasts,' their fine usher said
Here's to the lady who out of the blue
Gave us our characters, all of us too

With Gloucester's fine music, they all had a chance
At the reception to join in the dance,
And Dame Beatrix Potter said 'This is the way
I like to see all of you happy today.'

Joan Last

MY FATHER

An old oak tree stands alone in a wood,
Its roots are steadfast and sure.
Fixed to the earth like an anchor chain,
To stand the test of time.

A wise old owl sits in the tree,
In the heaviest branches, hidden in the leaves.
Watching the world go sailing by,
Viewing every moment with an eagle's eye.

Strong in character, sound in mind,
Never moves too early, he waits awhile,
This wise old bird, with a knowledgeable mind,
Reminds me of one who is patient and kind.

For his roots are strong and true,
Always gives an answer, correct and true,
Always held in the highest esteem,
By people he has met in places he has been.

To pay tribute to this man,
Is an honour for me,
For I must be the luckiest man in the world
To have a father who loves his children as much as he.

Andrew Brian Zipfell

To My Mother

She is a darling with an artist's eye,
That wondering, looks on Nature's store.
A glowing sunset or a windblown tree,
The fragile flower, the raging sea,
Are her delight.
Her voice like liquid notes sounds clear;
Gentle but strong in accents true.
Faithful and just, loyal, proud;
Kind but firm, with reassuring caring
Thought for others, generous to a fault;
Sharing in good times and in bad.
Patiently waiting by a bed of pain.
Humorous and full of joy.
Tragic happenings could never quite destroy her Spirit.

Noelle Hill

Tribute To 'Robinson' My Cat

Eyes alert and face so bright
   Sat upon my artwork on the right
      Ginger fur glistening in the sunlight sun
         Gallant warrior, full of fun
           Whiskers looking at me with grace
              Who runs away with my pencil at a pace
            Then jumps upon a sofa bed
              Where he rests, appearing dead.

Carol Bradford

A TRIBUTE

I had a friend,
he was the nicest man,
I ever knew.
In his presence, my spirit
would be refreshed anew.

Together, we were united
in true fellowship and peace.
There were times no word was spoken.
Yet communion, even in silence
would never cease.

Alas! He has gone now.
Released at last from all earthly woe.
When God calls,
we who are mortal
cannot say no.

In these last few years he suffered much,
Yet, never once did I hear him complain.
To see him suffer
caused a deep melancholy,
my soul to touch.

In harmony of spirit, we were as one.
Now it is my prayer that when time is done,
we will meet again, in that beautiful land,
many light years, far up there beyond the sun,
never more to part.
In eternity together, with all our loved ones.
Peace an joy forever we will share.

John Murray

TRIBUTE TO VERA

Tribute to Vera, a special lady
Her virtues were untold
But she took the hand of Jesus
And he gave her a heart of gold

Kindness was her password
Splendid her every deed
Always ready to befriend
Some lonely soul in need

When Jesus called her home
She left with a smiling face
Happy to meet her maker -
Saved by His loving grace

With serenity known by the saints alone
And a sparkle in her eye
Came the day of departing
'Twas hard to say goodbye

Looking at her picture now
How like Him she had grown
For His garden the good Lord has chosen
The sweetest and best for his own.

Norah Page

MY DADDY

You look like Victor Meldrew
And smell like a septic tank
You've had a sense of humour by-pass
And can't take a practical prank

You've got a head that wouldn't pass a Kwik Fit inspection
Your bum would fail an emissions test
You're really getting on in years
And you're almost past your best

You're more A reg than S reg
You're more a Skoda than a Merc
You keep having to go to the garage
'Cos the bits that ain't dropped off don't work

But you might be old and knackered
And nearly ready for the scrap heap
But call me sentimental
You're a dusty old relic I think I might like to keep

Gillian M Morphy

FOR KAY - ON HER 90TH BIRTHDAY

Each winter,
so many winters!
Kittens and puppies play
before the fire.

Each spring,
so many springs!
Horses and ponies stray
across the fields.

Each summer,
so many summers!
Roses and poppies grow
beside the lawns.

Each autumn,
so many autumns!
Music and friendship stay
to cheer the heart,

Each day,
so many days!
Memories pave the way
to peace of mind.

Jo Brookes

IAIN MACDONALD-MURRAY

A pipe major and
A brother to William.
Became the personal piper to
The Duke of Windsor.
A friend.
Taught him to play the pipes
And his own composition.
Had been a companion,
Took part in films,
'Marigold'
Then radio and television.
Became the resident piper of
The Scotch Huis,
A Scot by heart,
Much loved by everyone.

M MacDonald-Murray

WHO ARE OUR ANGELS?

How would we manage if there was no God?
Would we cope if He was not there?
The struggle and strain to live in this world
is sometimes too much to bear.

We can go to the churches to talk to our friends,
We get comfort from sharing our load.
I believe there are angels who help us along
Without them we never would cope.

I'm sure that God sends them, those wonderful folk,
who listen and try to erase
the pain and the suffering here on this Earth,
and turn difficult times to good days.

So thank you, dear angels that we cannot see,
We are grateful to know you are there.,
The knowledge that someone is listening to me
is proof there's an answer to prayer.

Doris E Pullen

A PHARMACIST WITH A DIFFERENCE

Status
Prestige
This job carries them both.
Is he just doing his job?
A question I ask time and time again.
For me he'll win my vote
For the pharmacist of all time
For he is patience, caring, knowledgeable
And his list of qualities goes on.
When doctors fail to cure my ails,
He cures them every time.
For the medicines he recommended
Worked all the time.
This news I shared with others,
They now told me I was right
This extraordinary man, of Indian culture
Has restored my faith in mankind.

Carolie Pemberton

MUM - A TRIBUTE

Eighty-six years on this earth
A babe in arms for World War One
Growing up between the Wars
Young wife you were as Two began

We three would surely not be here
Nor all your grandchildren so dear
Without your tender loving care
None of us would now be there

So looking back at my own life
From difficult birth to present day
Who gave me cakes on Friday nights
As I came home from school for weekend stay

Who nurtured my strong love of nature
Taught me many different things
Got me my first job from school
And the one today which brings
Enough money for my house
Where I live in contentedness

Who never moaned as I left for foreign parts
But kept me in her heart of hearts
Welcomed me when I returned
Knowing I had something learned

Who never said 'I told you so'
Whenever I was really low
Without my husband, just his child
And babysat when nights were wild

Kind and gentle to the end
You've always been my best friend
Sweet and caring all your life
You were good mother and good wife

Diana Price

Somebody's Son

We stand here with price and look up to this man
His achievements are many since his life first began
We have thoughts of a baby cuddly and warm
And the vows that we made to keep him from harm.

As a lad when he rescued the cat from a tree
Came running indoors with a graze on his knee
But there also were times when for courage he'd lack
When, with tongue placed in cheek we would have to sit back.

The morning arrived, he was just about four
A sturdy wee lad, not a babe anymore
School now filled his life and with friends he would play
Eager to learn something new every day.

The years swiftly passed - had they ever been there!
Now a handsome young man of compassion and care
University time - what an honour to be
Present the day he received his degree.

A happy occasion took place in his life
When a pretty sweet miss became his good wife
Now contentedly wed with a fine brood of three
There to continue our family tree.

His courage in danger could not be denied
On the day that a child could have cruelly died
So we stand here together, his old dad and me
See it justly bestowed - our son's OBE.

Our task now at end, been a pleasure to nurture
This character strong for his family's future
We give thanks to our maker, for 'twas part of his plan
To place in our care this dependable man.

Barbara Davies

EVEREST 1924

Frozen with time . . .
Endeavour with endurance lie
At the pinnacle of courage . . .
Sons of the most high mount,
Sleeping now but hardly then,
Counted with the best of men.
Metal from an English forge.
Swords sharpened on stone, to strike
The greatest marker ever known.
Conquerors at the mother breast,
Mallory with Irvine wrestled fate, to embrace
Astride that howling gate of Heaven but once to fall.
Ambitious climbers, who withal did stand the test by grace
And by God . .
On the face of it,
Such courage, side by side is blessed,
To now, in peace and
In memoriam,
Everest.

Roger Mosedale

MISS SMITH

Her beauty free upon the wind
No cares suppress her gentle mind
But petals fall from flowers sweet
And beauty leaves for oceans deep.

Her innocence in truth is white
For darkness endured made brighter her light
But petals fall from flowers sweet
And beauty leaves for oceans deep.

Her precious presence all around
Once lost, would not be found
But petals fall from flowers sweet
And beauty leaves for oceans deep.

But in the garden seeds are sown
And row on row flowers are grown.

Maxwell Anderson

THE GREATEST TREE OF ALL

From a seed, to a sapling
Grown with care, to a tree
Main branches stand tall
For all to see

Younger branches form
The tree becomes stronger
The roots of life
In the earth, grow longer

An anchor, held fast
To weather the storm
But try as we might
Some branches get torn

Autumn arrives, then winter
Leaves, rot in the ground
Slowly enriching the soil
Of the tree's surround

Our love, is the food
It brings strength to our tree
From a single seed, grows
A whole family.

Margaret Suffolk

LOUIS ARMSTRONG

Can there ever be another Louis?
The trumpet maestro, pinnacle of fame,
Who charmed his way into the hearts of millions,
Who hardly maybe even knew his name.

I was a privileged one at a performance
He gave in England once, - provincial tour,
Queuing for hours so as to gain admittance,
And still for years the memory will endure.

Stamping on stage to mark commencement
Sleepy time down South, signature strain
Snowy-white handkerchief, and clutching trumpet,
Satchmo, we shall not see your like again.

Except the statue of you in New Orleans,
In Louis Armstrong Park, sad and forlorn,
Your empty hand, no longer clutching trumpet,
Some vandal stole your very much-loved horn.

Ambassador extraordinaire, a colourful genius,
A great musician - worthy of his race,
Wonderful world, a thing of beauty,
He looked the whole world fully in the face.

Listen and marvel at the cadence,
Those busking ex tempore themes.
This is the stuff of jazz in all its glory,
Straight from the South - New Orleans and its dreams.

Leonard T Coleman

DADDY

My daddy was always my hero
I loved him and he was always there for me
He would listen patiently to all my wee stories
And he'd sing as I sat on his knee.
He was so happy and contented
So he was loved by everyone
He had a twinkle in his eye and was always telling jokes
Together we had so much fun.
From my very earliest memories
He was my guiding light,
He never lost his temper or even raised his voice
And he always made everything come alright.
Throughout the whole of my childhood
Especially through my teenage years,
He always gave good advice and listened
Then he'd calm me down and chase away my fears.
I was so glad that when I got married
We didn't live very far away,
And he got on so well with my new husband
So I still saw him or phoned him every day.
His great philosophy of life was really simple
Though, at times, it can be really hard to do
He said, 'You should always try to treat other people
The way you want other people to treat you.'
Now my daddy has been dead for more than thirty years
But I can still seek his guidance now and then,
I pray for him each day and in this special way
I always say, 'God bless you, Daddy. Amen!'

Mary Anne Scott

THE WAY IT WAS

She did not look for sympathy
She only looked for love
She did not seek publicity
She could not walk
Her wheelchair was the glove
That fitted the body of this little love
Handicapped, and yet with a smile
She would be taken each weary mile
People looked out for her, day by day
To have a wee word, to pass the while away
That was the way it was until
The day she passed away.
But for her closer family, the hurt was deep
As even though she could not walk
She such love gave, and a smile so sweet
Mongols, thalidomide, whatever they be
Have so much to give, to you and me
If we but take the time to see, and a friend of them make
For children are but children, for goodness sake
And is God not God of all
As into his arms he does them take?

M Lightbody

THE CHRISTENING

Since you were born, my darling child,
The world has seemed a better place,
Such is the joy you bring to us
When we behold your smiling face
And now you are to be baptised,
A tiny miracle of love,
Our fondest hopes are realised
As we give thanks to God above.

We've gathered here to wish you well,
And tell you that we'll do our best
To help you meet life's many trials
And comfort you when you're distressed
May you grow up to live in peace,
May God protect you day and night,
May you be strong and never cease
To fight for what you feel is right.

George Main

MUM AND DAD

They worked all day, and sometimes nights,
And they brought us up to do things right.
Dad worked his fingers to the bone
And Mum gave us a happy home.

Some people thought that we were poor;
They thought that they had so much more
With a telephone, TV and car.
But we were rich, richer by far.

'Cos we'd got wealth from Mum and Dad
A wealth some rich folks never had.
A wealth of love we shared instead
And we loved them well, but seldom said.

Letters we got, when they were gone.
Strangers confirmed what we knew all along.
Mum and Dad were special, not just to us
But to others whose lives they had barely touched.

'Cos they'd got wealth, our Mum and Dad
A wealth that some folks never had.
A wealth of love they shared instead
And we loved them well; but seldom said.

Rose Stedman

MY PET

Sad was the day when I had to call in the vet
To attend to my 'Mummy Squeaky', my beloved pet
She gave me so much love, affection and care
A feline tortoiseshell with so much devotion so rare.

For a lovely seventeen years she had given me all her love
A companion so faithful, a true gift from above
At night she would wait until I had settled in my bed
Then would climb onto my pillow and nestle close to my head.

When one is alone I love my cat's companionship.
My 'Lady Squeaky' would snuggle and I lay on my side and
                                                    sleep on my hip
Where would I have been without such devotion?
Such affection and love inspires all my emotion.

I loved my 'Mummy Squeaky', many tales I could tell
But at the end of the day she wasn't so well
We all have a life considered an adequate span
And within that time we do all we can.

My 'Mummy Squeaky' gave so much love to me
In return I loved her, fed her, but now she is free
Not just a moggie but special of a kind
A beloved pet that will forever and always remain in my mind.

Sometimes we take for granted so much and yet
The tears rolled down my face as she went to the vet
I knew it was time, the moment had come
'Mummy Squeaky' I loved you, you will always be number one!

I miss you so much, your furry coat like a fleece
But no longer in pain, for now you are at peace
RIP 'Mummy Squeaky,' thank you for all your love
I pray for your comfort in the other world above.

Tony W Rylatt

A SPECIAL PERSON

My mother is a special person.
She always gives you a loving
Welcome when you see her.

Always ready to listen
To any problems you may have.
Trying to help if she can.

Nothing is too much for my mum
Who really cares
And takes an interest.

It is nice to spend time with
My mum, who never rushes me.
Lets you take your time.

If I need to lie down
She understands.
When I am feeling quiet,
She knows I like to
Be left alone.

When I go for walks,
She often comes along.
These are lovely walks
We have together.

I have lots of nice memories
Spent with my mum.
Memories that will not fade.

Julie Smith

A VERY SPECIAL TULIP
(Written for my daughter, Grace)

You came into the world spontaneously and gave such joy.
We could never have known we had so much to enjoy.

Many said you were amazing,
so full of grace that left so many gazing.

You began to grow so beautifully and you had a will all of your own.
We were forever grateful for the way in which you had grown.

Yes, of course you were bright pink and at first you were so shy,
but as your petals opened so did your personality.
You became strong, so exotic, and the light that shone from within
touched everyone who came to look in.
There was never anyone with such vitality.

Your love was given freely to those who stood awhile,
but never more than to your family. Always ready with a smile.

You were so clever for someone so young
and so good at coping with whatever came your way.
You fought against the rain and gales and even thunder too.
Such a strong will to live a love of everything
that life and God gave you.

Then when your petals fall I still see your beauty
that maybe only I can see
but you are still a part of me.

Suddenly you are gone, just for a while,
until one day in springtime when again I see your smile . . .

Pam Smith

PRICELESS

For the love of it
Is what you say
For sheer hard work
From day to day
Giving every ounce
You have to give
Without question
This life you live

Priceless is what I say
For people like you with
So little pay
Endless patience
And time to care
This is a precious gift
You share

Appreciation is what
Comes to mind
This is lacking
You will find
Why oh why
When people like you
Are so deserving
And giving too

To those who employ
Such as you
Stop and think
Just what you would do
As without these gems
There would be
No you!

Wendy E Charlton

DEAR MUM

(Dedicated to Nachtar Kaur Rai - the best mother anyone could have!)

Who is always there for me?
> When I need someone to hold.

Who can help me get up?
> When I feel so low and cold.

Who helps me heal when I feel so bad?
> I can't help myself. I feel too sad.

Who helps me cope when things get too tough?
> I can't take anymore, I've just had enough.

Who helps me with homework when my sibling isn't in?
> Our love is so special and such a sacred thing.

I know who it is because there is no other,
> It can only be, my loving mother!

Sandeep Kaur Rai (14)

REQUIEM FOR A SCHOLAR

Love of learning and devoted years
Made him the scholar he became: research
Well found, exposition clear. His peers
Pronounced his treatises of lasting worth.

Flicking her dangerous, her fatal knife
The Fury, Atropos, in idle play
Indiscriminately passed his way
And cut the slender thread of sentient life.

May there be, somewhere, an Elysian field
Where knowledge learned minds have harvested
Is gathered in celestial mystery,
A treasury of wholeness that would yield
(As Plato dreamed and Aristotle said)
That stuff that lesser minds deem history?

William Speirs

LINDA FAIR (MCCARTNEY)

The lovely Linda is gone from our view
Well loved and respected by all that she knew
Gentle and kind - a wife and a mother
Loved by the family they wanted no other
Linda and Paul loved each other for many long years
Wherein they shared happiness and sometimes shared tears
Their children were their pride and joy
Three lovely girls the fourth one a boy
Togetherness, togetherness all that they shared
Just showed everyone how much they cared
Happy days spent riding the wind in their hair
Paul so dark-eyed Linda so fair
All over now Linda has gone to her rest
She shares company now with only the best
Sleep softly dear Linda - the beloved one
Well taken care of by the Father and Son
You'll long be remembered for all your kind ways
Your family will love you for the rest of their days

June Clare

TRIBUTE TO AFRICA, OH MY FATHER

Oh Africa,
Feelings run deep in the soul,
In the tragedy of the coal seam.
Time hisses and waits for no man,
Within the toil of Nature's loam.
Oh Africa and my father,
Forgive my very being,
For trespassing on thy soil,
So many centuries ago,
And know that deep within my soul,
I'm asking God,
That in the very schism of my anguish,
We might bestow, to thee a new Jerusalem,
Oh, Africa, great soul of Ghandi,

Born of Christ in man.

Elizabeth Rose French

BETTY

Farewell Betty. Our lives are richer for knowing you.
We will cherish your steadfast faith and prayer,
Of which the Lord is so fully aware.
May you rest in the sleep that is owing you.

Farewell Betty. We shall miss your Christian virtues.
Of your loving care and your service to others.
Of your tireless work for the Union of Mothers.
Surely your God will repay you your dues.

So much you leave behind. The words that were left unsaid.
Of the tasks that you started and are now left unfinished,
But for all you have done, let praise be undiminished.
It's too soon for us all when we're dead.

Farewell Betty. Rest awhile in the arms of the Lord.
In His Book of Life, your name is recorded,
And a free ride to Heaven you shall be afforded,
When our Lord Jesus comes and cries out 'All aboard.'

J G Ryder

HI PEANNIE!

You've loved me so much
That love seems betrayal
The word I mean.
The word love is not an
Adequate description of your love.
The four letters betray the depth
The scale and beauty.
Your love is all embracing
But only for me
And you
Together we are love
How will anyone ever know
We alone know.
No one will ever know our love
How smiling how close
How eternal and true
Made in Heaven
No one will ever know but us.

Simon Morton

BELOVED CLOWN

There are countless stars that shine
Past and present of eternal time
But the greatest star of all
For me, shone, blazed then died.

Indelible on my memory
Beloved Clown Prince of Comedy
No longer with us to delight
Dear Eric partner of *Ernie.*

Through all the early years and shows
We saw the changes as time goes
Grooming into the magic duo
Who brought us sunshine always.

The classic sketches still remain
Treasures to relive - again.
Those glasses and the paper bag
The slaps, the grins and silly laughs.

Famous people who gladly came
Enjoyed themselves and found more fame
Shirley and Angela, Andre too
Cliff and Glenda - to name a few.

Top hats and tails. funny overalls
They wore each well, as I recall
They were just as good, song or dance
Or in a favourite sit-com.

Dear Eric we will never forget
You, and the standards you have set
Together with *Ernie* you will endure
This year, the next - for evermore.

You would not want our tears of grief
Better by far, or tears of laughter.

Terry Daley

IF I COULD ISSUE MEDALS

This world holds many heroes
Both young and in their prime
Firemen fighting fires
Policemen solving crime
Nurses in our hospitals
With very little pay
Working long and hard
Each and every day
Doctors saving life
They do it all the time
Children helping pensioners
This really is quite fine
But I know of one fine lady
Who gave me so much time
She helped me to take the reins
Off this life that is now mine
She never does complain
You see she saved me from myself
It's hard just to explain
She helped me through a nightmare
That kept my soul encased
She showed me where the light was
My spirit she embraced
If I could issue medals
For heroes - here and now
I would have to give the biggest one
To my dearest friend - Gail Grinnell
Her faith has never failed me
She offers truth and honesty
This verse I write for her
A tribute of thanks from me

Jan Penn

LUKE

The door knocked and there he stood
A little ray of sun
So small and slight of frame was he
Full of mischief and fun.

'I've come to play at your house' he said
'My mum has gone away
Although I kind of miss her
I'm only here for the day.'

He sped through the house like a streak of light
Little bag of books discarded
With bird seed and watering can
Birds and plants were bombarded.

'Can I water them once more?
Now all the plants are fed.
What about the rhubarb?
It looks nearly dead.'

'Is there anything else that wants a drink?'
He struggles with the big can
Little puddles are everywhere -
'I'm working so hard Nan.'

'Let's get out the old game of catch
That your uncles used to play,
When they too were little boys
And it was a sunny day.'

'You've caught it Nan, you're very good,
You can have 20p.
Then if I catch it this time
It's a win for me!'

All too soon time has gone
'Here comes the other nan'
Big wet kiss upon the cheek
And up the path he ran . . .

Sue Sears

MUM

You cry when you're happy
You smile when you're sad
You keep your chin up
When you're feeling bad,
Your hands are magic
Your love is pure
You're my only one
And that's for sure,
You make me laugh
You make me good
You make me act
The way I should,
You are my pillar
You are my post
And when we're together
I'm at my most,
Thank you for your love
And for being a chum
But best of all
For being my mum.

Leanne Ditchfield (16)

JOYCE

Joyce, joy, a giver, oh! Such a blend
So gentle and caring, a lady, a friend.
I've known you so long
You've taught me so much
You have often inspired me,
I'm now able to touch -
True life without fearing,
Go forward each day
Your example in life,
To both work and play
Is a joy to behold,
Hold it for ever.
Joyce - what a name,
It suits you, how clever.
Don't ever change,
Never leave the joy out of Joyce.

Heather Agius

FATHER, I SALUTE YOU

Father, I salute you
you should have had a crown
for you helped everyone and anyone
when they were feeling down.

Father, I salute you
till the end you worked so hard
teaching your students Arabic
writing words on pieces of card.

Father, I salute you
you were so helpful and kind
as anything you'd do for us
you always said you didn't mind.

Father, I salute you
you truly were the best
the delightful, happiest, friendliest dad
may now in peace you rest.

Sabria Ragab (15)

A TRIBUTE TO NATURE'S HEALING POWER (OR THE DIFFERENCE NOW)

My body dangling oddly,
My hands so far away,
I felt I would lose my limbs
And just be a floating head.
So pulling my clothes down at the waist,
Trying to get back to body's centre,
The open spaces around me making me panic.
Half-closed eyes could help,
Calm consoled walking
Out to the sea with deep breaths
And slowly inland again, secure at coming to houses.
Those bad days are past, and now falling off my bike
With my hand ripped off,
Held just by a sliver of bone,
I can feel those fingers that once were so distant.
I shall keep my hand.
I relax to the healing power
Of Nature's living growth.

Tony Dixon

A Tribute To Poet R S Thomas Who Died On 25th September 2000

R S

You had hard things to say about Wales,
things that needed saying and
only you could say them.

It is safe now that you are dead,
tell us who those people were -
Iago Prytherch, Walter Llywarch, no good Dai Puw
and Cynddylan on a tractor?

'All Welshmen - and no Welshmen at all' you say?

You were an extraordinary poet yet you were
'an ordinary man of the bald Welsh hills,'
and now your glory 'in the sun's light that knows no setting.'

You were 'born on a blood-dark tide'
in Wales, which you said has
'no present, no future, only a past.'

It wasn't long before your mind was
'big with the poem soon to be born.'

But now, as we know from you, snow feels no pity,
'Your love is dead lady,'
poisoned by the 'treachery of the seasons.'

You are now free from the 'wantoner Welsh,'
'toppled into the same grave with oafs and yokels.'

May the air of your Heavenly Moor
break, as generous as bread, about your head.

Hwyl fawr!

Peter Davies

KIMBERLEY

Kimberley come back to me
I long for your caress
And all the things that we could be
My love I do confess

For you're the best I've ever known
And you alone can set me free
My heart and soul are yours to own
For now and all eternity

Kimberley if you could see
The way inside I truly feel
My music and my melody
My colours true reveal

My life before was just a war
I gave in to the night
I thought the ice would never thaw
I'd never see the light

Along you came a burning flame
My world was set on fire
A feeling I could never tame
Your love it took me higher

For none but you could pull me through
In you I found my sanctuary
The only love I ever knew
My life lives in you Kimberley

Sparky

GRANDAD, I WANT

Grandad, I want you to play a game with me,
    and I want you to stand just there.
Grandad, I want you to push me on my swing,
    and push me high into the air.
Grandad, I want you to run around and chase after me,
    because I can run fast now that I am over three.
Grandad, I want you to come with me and do the things that I say,
Grandad, I want you to stay with me and do not turn away.
Grandad, I want you to listen to me and push me high into the air.
Grandad, I do not know what you want, therefore I do not care.
Grandad, they say that you have gone and left me,
    to live in that heaven in the sky.
Grandad, I want you to come back to play some more games with me,
    for I never had time to say goodbye.
Grandad, I want you to come back to me, and stand here by my side.
Grandad, I want you to see me grow up and get married,
    and become a blushing bride.
Grandad, I know that you will not return to me from that Heaven in the
    sky, so I will just sit here a little white Grandad,
    and lower my head and cry.

C J Cross

FAREWELL TO BESS

Farewell, my well remembered friend,
For friend you were until the end;
Through rain and storm you followed me
Where traffic roared or wind blew free.

We met upon the moor that day;
You were a poor unhappy stray:
Man could not wish for love more true
Than that which I received from you.

I'd give the world to have you back
To tread with me the moorland track,
But I must keep the world instead,
For, Bess my poor old dog, you're dead.

Mervyn S Whale

MY FELLOW BEINGS

Thank you for the glory of the sun
Thank you for my good health
I have to get my duty done

I shall devote the hours
Of this golden day to you
By honouring your Holy Name
In everything I do

I will pursue my daily art
Without complaint or fear
And promise to be friendly
And sincere

I know there have been many a day
When I have whiled away
But this one I will make
Your special day
For all my fellow beings

So once more
Good morning God
Please depend on me
To honour you all eternity

Sabina Hill

THE SOUL SINGERS

Faces smiling
   ever shining,
Trusting - thankful
   for His care.

Blind to hostile hate
   so caring -
Sparkling love
   they long to share.

Through the dark a
   bright light glistens
They sing their 'Soul'
   in praise of God -

Joy of heart
   they know He listens
Following Jesus
   their Living Word.

Just like Him
   they suffer blindly
Mute to earthlings
   judging scorn.

For their strength
   their gift from Heaven -
From their hearts
   true Light is borne.

Mary Skelton

THE WORLD CHIEF SCOUT AND GUIDE

I was a Girl Guide dressed in blue
This is what we had to do
Serve the Queen - love our Lord
Keep our Promise and our Law

Trusty loyal helpful sisterly courteous kind
Obedient smiling thrifty - pure in word and mind

To do a good turn every day
Helping others on their way

Swimming camping on the hills
Earning badges for our skills

Meeting friends from foreign lands
Spreading goodwill shaking hands

Ninety years have come and gone
And the Movement still goes on

To Olave and Robert Baden-Powell
We must all say 'Thanks'
For allowing us so long ago
To join the Girl Guide ranks

They gave us so much pleasure
They gave us so much more
The memories we treasure
Our Promise and our Law

Anne Purves

TRIBUTE TO MY FIRST LOVE

Now and then I think of my childhood sweetheart,
Our youth and vitality we were never apart.
Young love, first love who can refrain,
The highs and lows the joys and pain.

Like yesterday I recall the birth of my children,
What excitement and fun we laughed so often,
I gave birth to a daughter and two sons,
They were three very individual ones.

I remember so well our deep love and bonding,
Our family as one always responding.
As a thief in the night came that evil day,
Death took my first love, we could not hold sway.

At times I look at my married siblings,
With wonderful partners caring and loving,
I see much of my first love in the way that they act,
They all have his genes and that's a fact.

I love to be with my grandchildren all six,
Five boys and a girl, what a mix,
They are part of my first love, he's part of them
I wish he had met them time and again.

I admit when I see my grandchildren smile,
Being together, laughing in a pile,
Their wit and charm all play a part,
In complementing granddad, my first sweetheart.

My whole life through, now and then I'll remember,
My first sweetheart and all the splendour,
He's give me through my three offspring,
Who gave me grandchildren what joy they bring.

Barbara Jermyn

2ND JULY 1972

(Katherine Jane Herring, in our hearts forever - Liz, John & David)

Once upon a summer's day
A princess she was born
Then suddenly on New Year's Eve
She left us quite forlorn . . .

This child did not have royal blood
In a palace she'd not live
I suppose the Lord just needed her
And for this we now forgive . . .

For although we do not understand
The workings of our God
We know that she is safe with him
In heaven up above . . .

I feel enriched for knowing her
I miss her smiling face
But in her leaving us so soon
She's left something in her place . . .

An aura that is always here
Like her arms around my being
I know that she is with me
'Cause true faith is without seeing . . .

Her friendship is a knot
That angel hands have tied
And I couldn't now forget her
However hard I tried . . .

Anne E Roberts

MEMORY

You're just a memory to me of all those good times
A memory so free they help me unwind
Feelings of love why did you go!
Come to me now honey, I'm feeling so low.

I don't want to hurt you, I don't want to fight
I just want to love you all over tonight.

Where are you now with some other chick?
You just want to hurt me baby, notch another tick
Can't you understand, it's you I'm looking for?
There's no one else I want knocking on my door.

I don't want to hurt you, I don't want to fight
I just want to love you all over tonight.

You make me feel that I'm the best
So why did you leave our love nest?
Come to me now honey, I'll show you some good love
You won't be sorry baby, you'll be so high above.

I don't want to hurt you baby, I don't want to fight
I just want to love you all over tonight.

Anne Farley

TO HONEY BUNCH

'Twas in the Spring you came to us
My darling Honey Bunch.
With eyes like almonds cased in gold,
And fur the softest pink.

How did you get thus far my love,
So hungry and so torn?
Yet something in your inner soul
Sang - go on, go on, go on.

'Twas on a morn we said goodbye,
Seventeen summers hence.
When He who sent you forth to us,
Had called you home to rest.

Margaret Carl Hibbs

A HERO'S WAR MEMORIAL

We place floral tributes in honour of so many brave women and men
Who fought and were slain for freedom's gain to win and reign
We wear special decorations to show none of you will ever be forgot
Our thanks is so inadequate but in heaven your reward is not lost
We view the many memorials and those cold granite stone slabs
Decorating the countryside where you fell such brave girls and lads
Many bear inscriptions so many have no names
All these are accounted for in heaven's brightness gleams

The enemy likewise are interred with these brave heroes
Seeing now the error of their ways as all friendliness glows
Here there is no language barrier all are one with the Lord
Who restored and made whole again according to His word
We pay our respects and offer our prayers and trust those who
                                                            interceded
Will pass on such messages omitting those cruel dishonoured deeds
Honouring as we do these brave men and women who fought to free
To make this life more beautiful our thanks O Lord to Thee

In that wondrous silence we hear as we pray
Thanking that Great Person who holds all in His sway
Then in this hush there is no more as we pass on our way
Remembering our sacred visit to this cemetery from which our thoughts
will never stray

R D Hiscoke

MARIOLOGY

Before her soul received its piercing sword,
Persuaded that, of women, she was blessed,
A maid, while virgin, humbly acquiesced
To bear a son, God's own incarnate Word.
There followed Census; Bethlehem, the ride
In fear to Egypt; Nazareth; the Kings.
How little Mary understood these things
Who lived to see her first born crucified.
What thought she then of God; of death; of birth?
Is she a Queen, as pontiffs claim, 'assumed'?
More like, in unknown ground she lies entombed,
Anonymously cradled in the earth.

Give thanks for one who, line of Adam's rib,
Gave birth to Christ and raised Him from the crib.

John M Beazley

THE NEW PUPPY

From out of the depths of sadness
You brought joy
And yet, your need was greater than ours,
You were homeless and unwanted
From out of that shared need
Blossomed a new, loving relationship
A new beginning
We offered you hope and a home
And you gave us love -
Unconditional!

Joan Thompson

JOHN WAYNE

For hours I watched the silver screen
As heroes came, then faded,
But not one! Fired emotions
That in me were long since jaded.

Then at last there came from way out west
A man who would rise to fame
And all other men would envy him
The one they called John Wayne.

This giant of a man stood tall
Not just in size, but pride
Back ramrod straight, jacket taut
Across his shoulders wide.

On screen he fought all evil
Defending what was right
And to the weak and the downtrodden
He was their guiding light.

To him they turned, their champion
On him they could rely
He had no fear of any man
Yet was not afraid to cry.

So from childhood to adulthood
True grit he did impart
And although he's long since passed away
He lives on in my heart.

Don Woods

FOR PETER

There is a man who is so dear.
I'm glad I can say I keep him near.
He keeps me safe.
He makes me feel strong,
I love him more than anyone.
With his dark brown eyes,
Which can see straight into my heart,
His big strong arms,
Which hold me when I'm hurt.
Those wonderful lips,
Which kiss me goodnight
This is the man who holds the key to my heart,
Who I will love forever,
Without a doubt.
I'll keep him close
Try and make him happy
I'll love him with all my heart,
Forever!

Lisa-Jane Clarke

CLOSE ENCOUNTERS

A tiny infant cradled close to a suckling breast,
a close encounter of nourishment and rest;
a time of togetherness for mother and child,
to lay content within those arms, lulled by her smile.

And so it is for us, with our Creator blest, for we
are held within Her arms, finding there our rest;
nestling close to the breast that gives life-giving food,
life that was outpoured for us upon that Holy Rood.

A time of refreshment, nourishment and love,
a close encounter of heavenly motherhood;
for all of us are children needing that love divine,
to be held within Your arms, knowing that we are Thine.

Catherine Riley

SIR TITUS SALT (FROM SALTAIRE IN YORKSHIRE)

I want to say how very glad
I went along to Saltaire.
A village in dear old Yorkshire
Heard about Sir Titus there.
He was a good employer
In those far off days,
Showed great compassion
For his work folk and their ways.
Daily toil in textile trade,
Work done at their best,
He provided good stone houses,
Leisure halls for their rest.
He gave not only work for living
But minds did evaluate,
Various skills and hobbies
Never to stagnate.
Today people still will visit
Go in the lovely church,
Again reminded of the man
Where he and his family rest.
So if you haven't been there
Go along to Saltaire
It's a joy to the heart,
To hear about a man who cared.

Mavis Catlow

My Shining Star

My youngest granddaughter is now seventeen
My daughter adopted her when she was two
'You are my grandmother,' she said
As I nursed her on my knees.

I looked into her big, blue eyes
They misted over with tears
She put her arms around my neck
I kissed her on her cheek.

You are my granddaughter Tracey
I love you with all my heart
No matter what you say or do
My love for you is true.

All through the years we have corresponded
We live many miles apart
I love you, I love you, she always wrote
My love for her just grows and grows.

I go to my daughter's house for holidays
Tracey stays by my side
They visit me every Christmas
Exchanging presents is such a delight.

Tracey is now a beautiful young woman
A credit to all the family
She is still being educated
Hasn't got a boyfriend yet.

Hetty Foster

A Tribute

Our country pays its Tribute to
The men in khaki and in blue
But there are others who deserved
A tribute for the way they served.

February 27th was a very special day
In our corner of Dorset, jet aircraft flew our way
Two Vampires and a Venom too
With thunderous roar above they flew.

To commemorate the old airfield
A plaque at Christchurch was unveiled
So that all the world could see
How we played out part in bringing Victory.

The planes flew past with a mighty roar
As I stood below and watched in awe
They circled round for all to see
And we were watching History.

We will never forget our debt to 'The Few'
Or the dedicated staff at *De Havilland's* too
Who designed and built the planes they flew
Which helped to bring peace for me and for you.

Where proudly now our houses stand
So we commemorate this land
The Fly Past by historic planes
Remind us all what we have gained.

J A Sida

AN ELEGY TO MY BEST FRIEND

You came when I was sad and bereft,
You came when there seemed nothing left,
You gave me strength to carry on
When I thought all hope had gone.
You encouraged me to start anew
And live a brave new life with you.

You helped me to enjoy again
The things I thought had gone -
Walks down a quiet, country lane
To see the sun come up at dawn.
Holidays beside the sea, a picnic in the wood
I enjoyed them all because you made me feel so good.

And now you too have gone
And I'm alone again once more,
But now I'm so much stronger than I was before.
You showed me how to live again
And so now I see
Although you've gone your influence, is still right here with me.

Pauline Anderson

MAHATMA GANDHI
(Written shortly after his assassination)

Your message lives through countless numbers
Of restless leaders toss in vain,
Your vibrant call awakes from slumbers
The Christian duty once again.

You were a dove in old man's guise
And rang so clear the bell of peace,
While all the rest was fraud and lies,
You fasted, and had conflict cease.

Still alive where hearts do yearn
Humble people sing your praise,
One day, master, we shall learn
To live out your holy ways.

Emmanuel Petrakis

HOMAGE TO JACKIE
(This poem is dedicated to the brilliant Jackie Collins)

I have read all your books
Full of psychotic crooks,
Romance, tragedy and gallantry, just look,
With twists and turns, some fantastic hooks.

Understandably you are a goddess of writing
Everyone finds your plots so inviting,
Because your stories are so exciting
There is always a mad rush for your books
That everyone is requiring.

Your humour is pure joyous laughter
Your style is sweet and sour,
And your protagonists have such righteous glamour
You're a madam that possesses great fiction power.

Your work just gets better and better,
And your quality continues to flower.
I look forward for your next novel to devour
For I enjoy reading your new works hour by hour.

I think your sauce is room for applause,
And your creativity deserves many awards
Respect is due for a maestro such as you,
Because you were educated at a university school
For, Jackie in this world your genius definitely rules.

Ali Sebastian

THE DAY I MET YOU
(For Valerie)

I'll never forget the day I met you standing there,
You stood in the opening at the neck of the woods,
Calm and peaceful and serene, you were like an angel.

A shaft of light passed through the streets behind you
And fell directly over your left shoulder, catching the light in your hair.
In front of you were scattered, autumn leaves on the ground.

Leaves that had started to turn a saddened, golden-brown colour,
they were like the colour of time that had been passed by.
They had faced the sadness and the test of time
and were wearily turning to face the long, hard winter months ahead.

As I looked up towards you your love and faith and hope embraced me
and I watched you look into my eyes.
And as our gaze met I saw my pain reflected in your eyes.
I saw my pain etched across your face.
The pain of my years passed by like a stream of sadness and sorrow.
Years and years of lost life, of lost youth, of lost love.

Then I was gripped by a sudden fear; had I come too late to this spot,
had I found you too late for myself?
I looked up towards you, my face grief-stricken, despairing,
and you gently bathed my wounded soul as only an angel would.

And you spoke to me saying 'You have come to me in this opening in
the wood where I have always been. I see your pain, I see your sadness
like the autumn leaves slowly dying and withering under my foot.
But I also see your future.
My orb of light will be your orb of light.
My font of happiness can be your font of happiness.
My love for myself can be your love for yourself.

I will always journey by your side until the remnants of your past have been dealt with. And when you have dealt with your past, I will still always be there for you. You can find me standing there, waiting, in the neck of the woods.'

Caroline Delancey

GRAN

When at me my old Granny smiles,
her face fills with wrinkles, miles and miles,
of lines put there by years of care,
but I can see the love that's there.

Her manner serene, and gentle at times,
when she thinks of my grandad who worked in the mines.
When she thinks how he passed, with his lungs full of dust,
how they'd lived up till then, lives of love and trust.

Now she gives all it seems to me,
her love, and her care to her family.
She cares not a jot, for her own well being,
always looking to see how others are feeling.

She's the one I can turn to when problems arise
puts me on the right road to go.
Won't laugh at foolish mistakes I make,
just says 'I've been there, I know.'

She's the hub of the family, our anchor in life,
the rock we all cling to through trouble and strife.
Gran, my gran, my wish if you'll give it,
may you be with me always, in life and in spirit.

Brian Toomey

FRIENDSHIP

Those golden times of summer shared
Long hours filled with pleasure.
Aladdin's cave, a casket filled
With memories to treasure.

Of heavy scented gardens
And petalled rainbow hues.
With leafy, shady blessings,
Remembered sweeping views.

A swiftly darting dragonfly
The muted humming bee.
The drowsy warmth of summer
Brought sweet tranquillity.

We strolled beside the waters
Of lakes and babbling streams.
Those days will be remembered
In the slumberous mist of dreams.

The chatter and the laughter
Carefree ease together.
The bonding of a friendship
That we knew would last forever.

Whatever else the future brings
Our friendship stands foursquare.
For in our hearts we know we'll hold
Our golden summer there.

Georgina McManus

BRIAN

He's a mischievous bundle of fur and fun,
The loveliest kitten under the sun.
He's black on top and white underneath,
And he scars my hands with his claws and teeth.

He doesn't miaow, but only squeaks -
I know what he means, for he almost speaks.
When I'm listening to music, he lies 'cross my knees,
Or he'll walk on my piano - kitten on the keys!

He's scared stiff of people, but me - he adores.
When visitors call, he prefers out-of-doors.
Then when they have gone and he comes back inside,
He's nervous no longer; there's no need to hide.

When I'm watching the telly he'll jump on my lap;
If he don't like the programme, then he'll have a nap.
While I put on a CD, he pinches my chair
And spreads himself out, so I can't sit there!

Now this, of course, just isn't done,
But it's only this young rascal's fun;
And if I stroke him as there he lies,
He'll smile at me with half-closed eyes.

This is my little bundle of joy,
And he knows he is 'Uncle's' boy -
A wonderful friend, as you can see
He knows that he will always be . . .
My Brian.

Roger Williams

FRANCIS LEDWIDGE

You see the writer's notebook,
You see the writer's pen.
You ask me where he's gone now?
He's gone with marching men.
He's gone to fight for good and right
With soldiers and with friends.
His notebook full of dreams and words
He'll never use again.
Tell me, tell me, why he had to go?
Tell me, tell me, tell me if you know.

The flower of youth with hearts of truth
And courage like a lion
Marched out that day, mere boys were they,
To slay and to be slain.
The poet and the farmer's boy,
The miner and the cook
Marched out into the canon's mouth
Without a backward look.
Tell me, tell me, why they had to go?
Tell me, tell me, how it happened so.

Now some will write and some will fight
And march with marching men.
His fate would choose them both: to use
The sword and use the pen,
To write with blood in grime and mud
And never write again,
And leave us wondering at the waste
And weeping at the pain.
Tell me, tell me, how it happened so.
Tell me, tell me, tell me if you know.

Kate Davis

To Louis

(Written after visiting the Writers' Museum in Edinburgh)

Inside the glass case they stand proudly on display -
A battered pair of boots last worn some Victorian day.
Beside them there is placed his hat, and his signet ring,
Worn perhaps, when he entertained the Samoan king.
A true romantic soul, whose goal lay within the southern seas -
His name was Louis, and he once owned all of these.
A century or more ago, the Teller of Tales sailed
Half-way round the world, where he settled and regaled
His loyal devotees with stories of his native soil;
Though many miles removed, to Scotland he stayed loyal.
Poetry and fable, adventure and romance,
Came flowing from the pen with which he wrote to make hearts dance,
And imaginations soar like they've not done before or since.
RLS was blessed with the gift to convince
Us, somewhere just beyond the quilted land of counterpane
Exists a place where each of us can be a child again . . .
His long hair blowing in the balmy, ocean breeze,
As Louis strides along the beach, home at last, at ease.
I seem to picture him the way, in the faded photograph
He looks with eyes a-sparkle, as if about to laugh.
And were I to concentrate I know my senses would be filled
With the sounds and sights of the home he set himself to build;
The sound of those very boots treading back and forth
On the veranda of Vailima, whilst to the north
A mighty mountain summit looms above the forest glade,
Where one day, beloved Tusitala shall be laid . . .
Now high upon the tree-topped mount, Louis is at rest
But I wonder, if all those years ago, he could have guessed
That the ring upon his finger, and the boots in which he stepped
One time many years from thence, would in a case be kept.

Jonathan Goodwin

IN MEMORY OF ROBIN FRIDAY

What demons stirred inside you Robin,
what made you so morose?
So that you were found after many days
dead from a heroin overdose.
Perhaps it's the nature of brilliance
that made you so unstable,
but many of us would have killed
to perform the skills of which you were able.
Your ghost still haunts us older fans
and now younger ones know your name,
you died at only thirty-eight but
achieved your hour of fame.
You arrived at Cardiff Central
and were arrested by the police
for not purchasing a ticket and
then of course came your party piece:
giving a keeper a two-fingered salute
plus a look of disdain,
yes, your ghost still haunts us older fans
and now younger ones know your name.
But what demons stirred inside you Robin?
You could have been a contender you know
and were not with the city for very long
but we certainly enjoyed the show.

Guy Fletcher

MY OLD FRIEND

Somehow, he has been here through thick and thin,
Helped me with ideas that I believe in.
And he has been my friend for many years,
Sharing always my laughter and my tears.

However, he never tries to change me,
Or tells me how different I could be.
Because he accepts me for what I am,
He's like a lion, while I'm like a lamb.

S Mullinger

TRIBUTE TO MY GRANDFATHER

Venerable friend, steadfast, true,
Down through the centuries
Your skilled hands poised, sensitive,
Standing proudly erect
Chiming melodiously
Reminding all of the hour
King of the house.

With what pride did your maker
Crown you with brass
Could you speak would you tell
Of Royal Pageants, Trafalgar, Waterloo,
Perhaps ask simply why
You are decked with holly each year.

Within your strong chest
A sturdy heart beating
On - ever - on
Into the future two thousand
And what?
New families, new centuries,
Sale or destruction?

Old man gazing out on the world
Unperturbed, unperturbable,
I salute you.

Patricia Weitz

EMELINE

Years ago, before I was born,
Man and woman, apart they were torn,
Man seemed to flourish, at such a fast rate,
Whilst women oppressed, were forced to wait,
Men worked hard, they went every day,
They thought that their women, just gossiped all day,
With education, the key to their cause,
They no longer wanted, their titles as whores,
Men felt women deserved no respect,
So political comment, they did not expect,
But one woman stood, feared not the malice,
She fastened herself, to Buckingham Palace,
Around her neck, she wore a note,
Demanding her rights, as an adult to vote,
Time has passed since that brave day,
Most of her followers, have petered away,
with political issues, abound to confuse,
She fought for your vote, the one you must use.

Geoffrey Woodhead

TO MY GRANDSON

He gurgles when he first wakes up,
And has a great big smile
He wriggles like a tiny pup,
But has to wait a while.

He greedily devours his milk,
That dribbles down his chin
His hair is fine, so soft as silk,
And has a cheeky grin.

When he's dressed he looks so neat,
He sometimes has a little weep,
We love him as he's very sweet,
Then rock him till he falls asleep.

Beulah Thompson

HEROES

Heroes invent the steam engine.
Heroes invade in wars.
Heroes are dark and handsome,
And covered in interesting scars.

But perhaps a braver hero
Knowingly spends his all,
To cover in concrete Chernobyl,
Or turn off the valve at Bhopal.

But all of these act in the knowledge
Of posterity judging them true.
Not struggling flies in flypaper.
Helpless, in thrall to the glue.

I give you unusual heroes.
The celibate pederast who,
Teaches his darlings companionship,
When for him it will never come true.

Or the man with the bad tempered invalid wife,
Who chooses to share in her pain.
And helps her go backwards a little bit slower,
With no possible hope for a gain.

Bill Waugh

YOU WERE THERE

You gave me hope when all hope had gone
You filled my dead, empty spaces with
words of faith and consolation
You fanned my dying spirit into life
and urged me on
You were there when everyone else had gone
You dried my tears and hushed my fears
You focused my eyes on reality and charmed
me with the beauty of nature
You instilled your peace in my soul
Your joy in my heart
With your message of love.
I just don't know how to thank you for all that.
Words seem inadequate
But they are all I have.
Thank you God.

Margaret Campbell

THINGS THAT MAKE ME SMILE
(In memory of my grandad)

His favourite rose bush 'Peace'
Nannan's special Sunday feast
A locket hung near where my heart beats
Down to the paper shop - treated to sweets
The pot in which his tea had been
The pets he used to help me clean
Pop into his favourite pub for a while

In memory of my grandad;

A simple, affectionate, remembrance *smile*.

Lindsey Fullwood (13)

TRAWLERMEN

Seas are raging,
Is God paging,
The trawlermen at sea?
Sons and fathers, family elders,
Are lost sad days at sea.

Model roles,
Search our souls,
To thank those farming on the sea.
Heartbreak, daybreak, the search is on,
Hope, for those missing on the seas.

Sometimes yes,
An SOS,
Unite stunned families,
Whose lives were nearly wrecked,
Association with the sea.

Do we take this might, with shallow draft?
With leisure, pleasure, and sailing crafts.
To horrify our forefathers,
Who were reverent of wild seas.
Their needs must, and justified,
For the food near stern and side.
With pride and fear, some paid life's fee,
The trawlermen at sea.

So let's pray for help and safety,
Appreciation, hope and honesty,
Becalmed or storm,
As life may be,
The trawlermen at sea.

Barrie W Neate

SUBMISSIONS INVITED
SOMETHING FOR EVERYONE

POETRY NOW 2001 - Any subject,
any style, any time.

WOMENSWORDS 2001 - Strictly women,
have your say the female way!

STRONGWORDS 2001 - Warning!
Age restriction, must be between 16-24,
opinionated and have strong views.
(Not for the faint-hearted)

All poems no longer than 30 lines.
Always welcome! No fee!
Cash Prizes to be won!

Mark your envelope (eg *Poetry Now) 2001*
Send to:
Forward Press Ltd
Remus House, Coltsfoot Drive,
Peterborough, PE2 9JX

**OVER £10,000 POETRY PRIZES
TO BE WON!**

Judging will take place in October 2001